DRAWINGS BY GEORGE ROMNEY

FROM THE FITZWILLIAM MUSEUM
CAMBRIDGE

FITZWILLIAM MUSEUM
CAMBRIDGE

DRAWINGS BY
GEORGE ROMNEY

Exhibition selected and catalogued by
PATRICIA JAFFÉ

CAMBRIDGE UNIVERSITY PRESS
CAMBRIDGE
LONDON · NEW YORK · MELBOURNE
FOR THE FITZWILLIAM MUSEUM
CAMBRIDGE

Published by the Syndics of the Cambridge University Press
The Pitt Building, Trumpington Street, Cambridge CB2 1RP
Bentley House, 200 Euston Road, London NW1 2DB
32 East 57th Street, New York, NY 10022, USA
296 Beaconsfield Parade, Middle Park, Melbourne 3206, Australia

First published 1977

Printed in Great Britain at the
University Press, Cambridge

Library of Congress Cataloguing in Publication Data

Romney, George, 1734–1802.
    Drawings by George Romney.

At head of title: Fitzwilliam Museum, Cambridge.
1. Romney, George, 1734–1802. I. Jaffé, Patricia.
II. Cambridge. University. Fitzwilliam Museum.
III. Title
NC242.R64J34   741.9'42   77–8080
ISBN 0 521 21766 0 hard covers
ISBN 0 521 29270 0 paperback

PREFACE

'George Romney (1734–1802) is accepted by common accord today as next after Reynolds and Gainsborough of the portrait painters before the age of Lawrence . . . Like Gainsborough, Romney was always complaining about the drudgery of face-painting, and we have the evidence of Flaxman (who became his friend only in later life) that "his heart and soul were engaged in historical and ideal painting", yet there is little to show for this save a mass of drawings for high-flown compositions, mostly in the Fitzwilliam Museum at Cambridge, and one or two unsatisfactory pictures for Boydell's Shakespeare Gallery of 1787 onwards.'

The words are those of Ellis Waterhouse in his *Painting in Britain 1530 to 1790*, first published in 1953. His reference to 'a mass of drawings' in the Fitzwilliam soon attracted more enquiries than the exiguous staff of the Museum could cope with. In 1957 a trainee-assistant, a recent graduate of the University, was engaged to prepare in one year catalogue entries for these drawings, some of them intended for portraits as well as many for 'high flown compositions', about 600 in all. Within the limits of practicability this task was completed on time, the limits being those of opportunity to travel and to study comparisons at first hand. Over 5,000 authentic drawings by Romney survive, scattered widely from London to Paris and Chicago to Cape Town: but the Fitzwilliam, starting with the Reverend John Romney's gift in 1818 of a careful selection of his father's drawings, has acquired the largest share.

It is particularly fitting, twenty years after this long overdue start to scholarly investigation of its Romney holdings, that the Fitzwilliam should have been able to invite its former trainee-assistant, Patricia Milne-Henderson, now Patricia Jaffé, to select and catalogue an exhibition. She has had in the meantime opportunities to extend her researches, and in part to make them known. In the U.S.A. she was a Fellow of the Folger Shakespeare Library (1959–60); she catalogued the Dilworth Collection of the Yale University Gallery (1960–1); and, while Acting Director of the Smith College Museum of Art in Massachusetts (1961–2), she organised and catalogued *The Drawings of George Romney*, which was the first and hitherto the only important exhibition to be devoted to the theme. In the two years following her return to Cambridge as a Research Fellow of her College, Newnham, she took up again the problems of the Fitzwilliam's drawings in the context of her wider experience of Romney's work and interests. Her *Romney* of 1966, in the series 'I Maestri del Colore', and her catalogue of *Lady Hamilton* for the Kenwood exhibition of 1972, published some of her findings and assessments. More come out now with her choice from the Fitzwilliam's drawings and with her running commentary, printed in the catalogue, on what she has chosen.

Occasion has been taken to lift drawings from the John Romney Album. For this delicate undertaking we are fortunate in having at hand in the Museum's studios the skill of the A.M.S.S.E.E. conservation specialist, Miss Doreen Lewisohn. Thereby a number of drawings by Romney have come to light, on the backs of his drawings, account of which is taken for the first time by Mrs Jaffé's catalogue. The publication of this has gone forward under a new, very welcome arrangement between the Syndics of the Fitzwilliam Museum and the Syndics of the University Press. To enrich the illustration, the Paul Mellon Centre for British Art and British Studies has made a handsome grant. We are grateful also to the Arts Council of Great Britain for arranging a 1978 tour of the exhibition to Kenwood and to other centres, outside London, so that it can be enjoyed far beyond Cambridge in the year following its showing here. A guarantee of support from the Arts Council with regard to sales of the catalogue means that copies will be available to the public throughout the projected tour as well as at the Fitzwilliam.

The prime showing of the exhibition in our Adeane Gallery is offered as our principal contribution to the Visual Arts Programme of the 1977 Cambridge Festival. As a way of sharing with the City and with its multitude of summer visitors the pleasure and interest of the Museum's still too little known collections, *Drawings by George Romney* takes its place in succession to the bicentennial exhibition offered by us to the 1976 Festival: *John Constable: drawings and watercolours*, which continues on tour through the good offices of the Arts Council. Once again the Cambridge Festival Board has encouraged us to go ahead with a project well beyond our ordinary means; and once again we count thankfully and trustingly upon a substantial subvention towards the costs of the exhibition, and upon full support for a special public lecture on its theme, to be given in the Museum on 23 July by Patricia Jaffé. Her we thank above all for her generosity in giving her services in the selection and cataloguing of this exhibition, tasks which she has the best claim to perform.

Cambridge 1977   MICHAEL JAFFÉ
                                                        Director

PLATES

ACKNOWLEDGEMENTS

Over the past twenty years scores of kindly people have helped me to pursue Romney's drawings. It would be very difficult to list every one; the fear would be that someone had been omitted. The body consists of private collectors, the staffs of libraries and museums, photographers and dealers, both in Europe and in the United States. Only the bare bones of this support can be indicated here.

J. W. Goodison comes first. He gave me the job of cataloguing the Fitzwilliam Romney drawings. The English Speaking Union is next. They gave me a scholarship enabling me to do further research in the United States. There my greatest debts are to the Folger Shakespeare Library, and to Mr and Mrs J. Richardson Dilworth who made available their enormous collection, now part of the Yale University holdings. My memory of the thousands of drawings I have seen could not have been held together without photographs acquired with the aid of a grant from the Penrose Fund of the American Philosophical Society. Newnham College had the imagination to support Romney studies by giving me the first Research Fellowship at a woman's college in this university to be held by a student of the History of Art.

Finally I have to thank the present staff of the Fitzwilliam Museum, and my immediate family: in particular, Frances Lee who has cheerfully typed sometimes difficult manuscripts, and Magdalena Rosak whose help with my young children has given me time to attend to the writing of this catalogue.

PATRICIA JAFFÉ

When in 1816 Richard, 7th Viscount Fitzwilliam of Meryon, died, a bachelor, he bequeathed to the University of Cambridge his paintings, prints, books, illuminated manuscripts and holotype music. He also left £100,000 in South Sea Annuities with which to build a Museum to house this noble collection. His University, which had never had an art collection of any kind, deliberated. The novelty was great. Fortunately they accepted the bequest, thereby inspiring others to make further donations; one of these was a former Fellow of St John's College, the Rev. John Romney, son of the painter. As George Romney's only surviving child, John had inherited his father's entire estate. In 1816 he still retained much that had remained in the Hampstead studio at the time of his father's death. The idea that a selection of the virtually unknown drawings should be added to the Cambridge collections pleased him. He must have set about gathering an appropriate group, and making a manuscript catalogue, almost as soon as he heard that Lord Fitzwilliam's bounty had been accepted. One hundred and sixty-four drawings were offered to the University in 1817. Again they deliberated. In 1818 they formally accepted the gift. The drawings and the catalogue together provide the corner-stone of studies of Romney's subject pictures. The collection was increased in 1874 by buying *en bloc* several hundred more drawings. Since then notebooks, sketch-books and single sheets have been added by gift, bequest or purchase. The present exhibition includes drawings from every category.

John Romney, the precipitate product of a hasty marriage which occurred in October 1756, only six months before his own birth, was never on such terms with his father as to be privy to all his artistic plans. Yet he rightly saw his father's drawings as the key to understanding his fancy subjects: 'It was a regular custom with Mr Romney to make sketches for his principal works, and as most of his sketch-books have been preserved, every picture of importance that he painted and many that he intended may be traced in them almost in chronological order. Upon some occasions so many different modes of representing the same subject presented themselves to his fancy, that he made several studies either varied in part or in whole, and executed in a slight bold and rapid manner just sufficient to convey the ideas and from these he afterwards made his selection' (J.R. 54–5). John Romney's was a privilege which can never more be enjoyed. That unbroken series of sketch-books has scattered like a string of beads snapped on a pebbly shore. Many have gone leaving barely a clue to their existence, separated and split on the art market during the past hundred years. So his identifications are set aside at one's peril.

There are, however, areas hardly touched upon in the John Romney Gift. These belong particularly to the end of George Romney's life when Revolutionary sympathies, encouraged by such friends as Tom Paine, William Hayley, the Rev. John Warner and William Blake, begot enthusiasms and interpretations in his art which could have marked him a dangerous radical. After 1794 all concerned for his reputation saw to it that references to the radical aspects of his art remained unpublished. Even in 1816 John Romney continued to shield his father's political reputation. At the time of Romney's death in 1802 public opinion in Britain, embroiled in the Napoleonic Wars, was super-sensitive. Perhaps it was fears that public reactions might have been adverse had the contents of the painter's studio been revealed too soon, or in their entirety, which caused the long delay in arranging a fashionable auction of his effects. Before that

I

happened there was, of course, a quiet house-clearing auction up at Hampstead. Friends and sympathisers were allowed to survey the range of works in the studio, and also those retained for later disposal. Prominent among these friends was William Blake who went to look through the canvases stored with Saunders, Romney's old frame maker (Blake to William Hayley, 26 October 1803 – Nonesuch p. 831). Blake's reactions were enthusiastic. He wrote appreciatively of 'engraving after Romney, whose spiritual aid has not a little conduced to my restoration to the light of Art'. (Blake to William Hayley, 23 October 1804 – Nonesuch p. 852). It was in 1804, and Blake was working on the print which he called *The Shipwreck*. Practically no drawing of this subject, and no full composition by Romney, is known. It is significant also that no sketch for *Woltemad on horseback rescuing survivors from a shipwreck at the Cape of Good Hope*, nor for *John Howard visiting prisons and lazarettos*, nor yet for the apocalyptic scenes of *The Fall of the Damned*, inspired by Milton, were included in the fashionable sale of 1807 at Christie's. Certain subjects depicting distress, disaster and domination were taboo. In the middle of the Napoleonic Wars they must have been thought demoralising. Fortunately at least some drawings of Howard subjects and of scenes from Milton survived in the family until 1816, and were among those presented to Cambridge. Moreover, subsequent purchases have helped to fill the gaps. By surveying the Fitzwilliam Museum collection as a whole, we can catalogue the most important subjects and events of Romney's working life.

This is not the place for his biography, but a glance at his family background helps to explain much of his later life. He was born at Beckside, on the outskirts of the little town of Dalton-in-Furness, Lancashire, on 15 December 1734. He had an elder brother and sister; and he was to have eight more brothers before he was fifteen. The father of this large family was John, a joiner and cabinet maker who had on occasion to turn his hand to carpentry, but who managed to build up a good country business. He seems to have had some engineering skills, and to have been a genuinely inventive countryman who farmed his small freeholding with skill and imagination, introducing improved methods. Although he was a literate man, with a love of books, his was not a way of life in which learning was paramount. Only William, his eldest son, was given anything more than a scanty education. George's schooling by the Rev. Mr Fell at Dendron is said to have ended at the age of twelve, when he was brought home to help with his father's business. The family had moved from Beckside when George was eight, to settle on a small estate, Upper Cocken: probably the greater labours entailed in running this larger property prompted the second son's recall. Indeed it may have been a time of crisis for his mother, who had had eight children by then, who was pregnant again, and who, probably, this time, was ill. In July 1747 she was to bear sickly twin sons who died soon after birth. To George his family may have seemed suffocating. He was later to reject all normal family ties.

Thanks to the good offices of Mrs Gardner, sister of a business colleague of his father's, and the lady with whom he had lodged when away at school at Dendron, George was eventually allowed to abandon his father's business for art (J.R. 12). Mrs Gardner in her turn was to have a son, Daniel, sixteen years younger than Romney, who became a portraitist, and even attended the Academy Schools. Daniel probably inherited his visual sense from his mother, who had had sensitivity enough to recognise George's talent. Apart from her encouragement, George may have relied chiefly on books for his early inspiration. The

Fitzwilliam owns his copy of Leonardo da Vinci's *Treatise on Painting* (London, 1721), four times inscribed with his name and three times with a date, 1754, 1755 and 1769. Its pages are liberally spread with thumb marks and paint smears. Another book, in which he is known to have written his name and the date 1755, is Le Brun's *Passions* (J.R. 11). 1755 was a significant year for him. On 20 March old John Romney, bowing to the persuasions of his son, and to informed opinion, allowed George to sign indentures, apprenticing himself for four years, for the sum of £21, to the itinerant artist Christopher Steele. Master and pupil travelled as far as Kendal and set up their temporary practice: but the swash-buckling Steele also courted a young lady and inveigled her into eloping to Gretna Green. It was neither what Romney had expected, nor what he had been used to: he found himself left to placate the girl's family, his Master's creditors and the unsatisfied clients whose portraits remained to be finished. The young apprentice was overcome. According to Hayley, he fell ill with a fever (W.H. 21). The results for Romney personally were disastrous, whatever may have been the success of the portraits he finished off. Nursed back to health by his landlady's daughter, Mary Abbot, a young woman seven years his senior, he was lured into a liaison from which he was not allowed to escape. To make matters worse, Steele, who found Kendal too hot for him after his marriage, had gone on to York and ordered his apprentice to join him. Mary Abbot was pregnant: she and George hurried through a face-saving marriage on 14 October 1756, before George left. It was a curious alliance from the start: Master and apprentice remained over nine months in York, while the new Mrs Romney waited in Kendal. The baby, John, was born on 6 April 1757. Romney and Steele did not return until the late summer. Even then the Romneys had little chance to consolidate their marriage. The painters again left Kendal, this time for Lancaster. There is no evidence to suggest that Mrs Romney ever made any attempt to join their itinerant life, even after Romney in the last months of 1757 had bought himself out of his apprenticeship and began to carry on business on his own account. In the next five years, before he set out for London in March 1762, Romney returned to York and Lancaster, worked in Manchester and even as far south as Cheshire. He did his best to support his wife and son, and although in 1760 they had another child, a daughter, their family life never seems to have been ecstatic. For George at least, these were years of grind, both in seeking commissions and in executing them. Very few drawings or subject pictures survive from this period.

Those that do show an unsophisticated naiveté evident in the first items of our exhibition.

1 Romney's Wife

Two sheets mounted side by side, both brown pastel with slight touches of black on pale cream laid paper.
1a. 204×159 mm (8×6¼ ins.); 1b. 204×160 mm (8×6$\frac{3}{16}$ ins.)

PROVENANCE: Given by C. Fairfax Murray, Esq., November 1917
(902 a & b)

Kenwood, 1961, Nos. 42 and 43. (Since then the drawings have been lifted from their old mount and rematted, revealing holes from stab stitching down the right hand side of 902b. 902a has stilus marks on the *verso*, evidently one stage in tracing off the head so that it could be drawn on another sheet, excluding the hand. 902a has no stitching holes, but must have been cut out of the sketch-book close in to the binding.)

Romney left Kendal, and his wife, in 1762. Almost seventy years later, his son John gallantly tried to refute the widely held belief that Romney deliberately abandoned his wife and children: 'As a proof that he entertained no such intention, he came twice afterwards to see his wife' (J.R. 35). But from the evidence we have it seems likely that any portrait drawings of Mrs Romney were made before 1762. She would then have been 35; and the present drawings would seem to be of a woman no older than that. John, who presumably knew her best and certainly wished to show her in the best light, describes her: 'She excelled more in symmetry of form, than in regularity of features; yet in this latter particular she was far from deficient' (J.R. 16).

2   King Lear Asleep

Pencil strengthened extensively with black chalk
343 × 532 mm (13½ × 20¹⁵⁄₁₆ ins.)
Verso: inscribed 'No. 123' in ink. Pencil sketch of the same group as *recto*, Cordelia bending further forwards

PROVENANCE: B.V. 7

This is included by John Romney among the 'sixteen studies which were made during Mr Romney's residence at Rome, and soon after his return to England' (J.R. 257). But the anatomical uncertainties and likelihood that the composition is a pendant to *King Lear Awakened by his Daughter Cordelia* which appeared in the 1762 Lottery (J.R. 24) suggest that this may be of an earlier date. The subject is from Act V of Nahum Tate's adaptation of Shakespeare's tragedy, in which the play is given a happy ending.

> Romney's simple ambition was to be a great painter. It was the lure of learning as much as that of fame and profit, that drew him to London. Having made £100 on the Lottery of 20 of his subject pictures and copies, he left Kendal for the week long ride on 14 March 1762. Once settled in the capital, he concentrated on building up his practice, establishing his reputation for imaginative compositions as well as portraits, choosing subjects such as *The Death of David Rizzio* (1762) and *Samson and Delilah* (1764). Above all his aim was to improve his art. His studies did not allow him to return home for years. Even London was not the centre of the art world. With an old friend from the Dendron School, Thomas Greene, he set out for France on 30 August 1764. Greene kept a diary of their tour (I am indebted to Greene's descendant, the Dowager Countess of Lichfield,

for permission to work on this MS). From it one can plainly see that Romney's life was already very different from that of the itinerant apprentice who had married Mary Abbot eight years before. They took tea with ladies, listened to the harpsichord in private drawing rooms, visited Greuze and were guided through the art collections of Paris by Vernet. They returned to London in early October: but it was not until the autumn of the following year, 1765, that Romney found time to revisit his family in the north. Two years later he paid his second visit. The little daughter had died in 1763, but his son John was now ten, and already storing up information about his increasingly famous father. This time he noticed how much Romney's work had improved since 1765 (J.R. 53). It was the last visit the schoolboy ever remembered his father making.

In London, thanks partly to introductions from Greene and other friends, Romney was beginning to make a name for himself. In 1768 he exhibited a large portrait of the numerous Leigh family (now National Gallery of Victoria, Melbourne: Felton Bequest). In 1769 he exhibited *The Warren Family* (see subsequently cat. nos. 11–14 below), a great public success. In 1770 he capped that triumph.

3 Melancholy

Pen with brown ink and brown wash over pencil on buff paper
508×308 mm (20×12⅛ ins.)
Verso: inscribed '130' in ink

PROVENANCE: B.V. 26

Having exhibited with the Free Society of Artists during his first years in London, Romney transferred his allegiance in 1770 and 'exhibited with the Chartered Society in Spring Gardens. To the catalogue of this Society, in the above mentioned year, he contributed two pictures – one representing a female in the character of *Melancholy*, and the other, in that of *Mirth*. These personifications were borrowed from the poetic fancy of Milton, as displayed in the exquisite poems of L'Allegro e Il Penseroso' (J.R. 61). In the check list of drawings given to Cambridge, John Romney correctly identifies this drawing as 'Pensierosa'. It can be compared with sketches for the same work in a sketch-book belonging to a private collector in Pennsylvania. There were also numerous sketches in a sketch-book which was part of the De Pass collection at the Royal Institute of Cornwall, Truro. In the Chartered Society's exhibition catalogue, the finished paintings appeared as Nos. 112 and 113, *Mirth* and *Melancholy* respectively. John Romney comments, 'These pictures had great merit. The drapery of Melancholy was particularly fine; its forms were broad and grand, and executed with such gusto that Mr West, many years after, complimented Mr Romney by saying it was equal to Raffaelle' (J.R. 63).

To paint figures in comparative repose was one thing. To show them in that state of high animation so necessary for dramatic pictures, needed anatomical knowledge. Romney's knowledge was shaky: the relation and indeed proportion of his wife's hand, head and shoulders in cat. no. 1 are poor; in cat. no. 2, the hang of Lear's arm is dislocated and the definition of the other limbs imprecise; in *Melancholy*'s companion, *Mirth*, the figure of the dancer is cunningly swathed in folds of voluminous dress and draperies. England offered few opportunities for life studies. Like many students, Romney chose the next best thing, study in the Duke of Richmond's gallery of casts (Chamberlain 43). Italy, by contrast, offered the originals of those casts, a wealth of art collections and a climate warm enough to tempt models to undress with less reluctance. Moreover intellectual snobbery deemed that a man could more easily succeed as an artist if he had travelled. France behind him, Romney's sights were set on Rome.

Ozias Humphry, the miniaturist, had been lodging in the same house as Romney, and resolved to accompany him. Humphry planned the journey, writing to Nathaniel Marchant in Rome to ask for suggestions on the best route and advice about accommodation (Royal Academy, MS I/126). On 20 March 1773 the two left for Italy. By the end of April they had reached the south of France. Arriving in Nice on Sunday 2 May, they delighted in seeing Maypoles with the local women 'hand in hand, dancing round them like *The Hours of Guido*, and singing beautiful airs; their movements were sometimes very slow and increased gradually till they became very quick; then they were slow again; they were perfectly in time with one another, and moved with the greatest vivacity and spirit: the air of antiquity it carried along with it had the most enchanting effect. I thought myself removed a thousand years back & a spectator of the scenes in Arcadia.' (George Romney to Thomas Greene, draft journal letters in a notebook presented to the Fitzwilliam Museum by Charles Fairfax Murray in 1917: quoted in an emended form by J.R. 83.) For Romney the antique was coming to life before his eyes. Once in Rome both life studies and the antique were more readily available than in England.

4 Nude female model half reclining

Black chalk worked with stump, strengthened with black chalk, and heightened with white on buff paper
479 × 403 mm (18⅞ × 15⅞ ins.)

PROVENANCE: Portfolio 1112

From a portfolio of twelve drawings of the female nude. All have been folded in half (at one time), possibly for ease of transport. These careful, rather academic drawings are presumably the result of Romney's life studies in Rome. 'There was at that time a young female of fine form, who lent herself to the artists for hire as a naked model, and by these means supported herself and her mother ... Mr Romney availed himself of so favourable an opportunity for studying the *nude* and made many sketches from her; he thus acquired an accurate knowledge of the female form in all its diversities of attitude' (J.R. 97). The Fitzwilliam series of studies seems to be of a private model; the view-point from which the pose is studied is always the principal one. No student at a life class could have hoped to have such luck consistently.

The pose of this particular drawing shows appreciation of Boucher and the art of mid-eighteenth-century France.

5 Nude female model posed as a dancer with cymbals

Black chalk worked with stump, strengthened with black chalk and heightened with white on buff paper
520 × 394 mm (20½ × 15½ ins.)

PROVENANCE: Portfolio 1113

See notes on cat. no. 4 above. Romney's choice of a dancing pose for his nude model is significant, after his trials with such a figure in *Mirth* and his appreciation of the May Day festivities of the women in Nice.

6 Venus and Adonis

Charcoal
371 × 540 mm (14⅝ × 21¼ ins.)
Verso: charcoal, profile directed to left, mouth cancelled, possibly for *Medea*. Numbered in ink '127'

PROVENANCE: B.V. 3

This is included by John Romney among 'sixteen studies which were made during Mr Romney's residence at Rome and soon after his return to England' (J.R. 257). As we possess very few sketch-book notes from the Roman period, it is to be presumed that Romney in Rome generally worked on this larger scale. The identification of subject is John Romney's. The story of Adonis, and of Venus's love for him is told in Ovid's *Metamorphoses*, Book X.
(Ovid, *Metamorphoses made English by Several Hands*, London, 1733 Vol. II, p. 53)

7 Two lovers

Charcoal
376 × 548 mm (14¹³⁄₁₆ × 21⁹⁄₁₆ ins.)
Verso: charcoal, *Jupiter:* (cf. B.V. 5); inscribed 'No. 13' in ink

Again among the 'sixteen studies' grouped by John Romney as products of the Italian trip, this was probably conceived as a pendant to cat. no. 6 above, the rôles this time reversed. Nearly all the drawings in this group of sixteen show the nude in some aspect, and it is evident Romney's confidence to treat the human body was evidently increasing.

8 A personification of sorrow

Pen with brown ink over pencil
451 × 267 mm (17¾ × 10½ ins.)
Verso: pen with brown ink; composition sketches for a woman with two children; inscribed in ink '138'

PROVENANCE: B.V. 32

Tentatively identified by John Romney as 'The Damsel from the Ballad "Twas when the seas were roaring" or perhaps a personification of sorrow', this is related in technique and morphology to other sketches of a pensive woman in the volume containing notes on processes of painting, etc., kept by Romney in Italy, presented to the Fitzwilliam Museum by Charles Fairfax Murray in 1917.

9 Ceyx and Alcyone

Pen with brown ink over pencil
333 × 454 mm (13⅛ × 17⅞ ins.)
Verso: pencil sketch for the figures of Ceyx and Alcyone in reverse. The body of Ceyx and head, arms and knees of Alcyone correspond exactly with the drawing on the other side; the line of Alcyone's back has been changed. The *recto* appears to have been traced through with the sheet held to the light.

PROVENANCE: B.V. 9

Again one of the 'sixteen studies' identified by John Romney as having been made in Rome or soon after his father's return to England, this relates stylistically to cat. no. 8 above, and compositionally to a charcoal sketch formerly fol. 12 in a large sketch-book from the collection of the late Professor Isaacs of London (Sotheby's, 20 March 1963, lot 13; subsequently broken up by a dealer). This sketch-book could be dated on internal evidence 1775–8. No doubt Romney in the first months after his return to England had fewer sitters, and more leisure than later in his career. He was thus able to continue work on subjects he had projected in Rome.

The story is from Ovid's *Metamorphoses*, Book XI. '*Ceyx*, perplex'd with the prodigies of his family, resolves to go and consult the Delphian oracle; from which voyage he is strongly persuaded by his queen *Alcyone*: He, however, pursues his resolution, and is drowned in a storm; she in his absence begs she may know his fate in a dream...' The body of her husband is swept to her feet by the waves. (Ovid, *Metamorphoses made English by Several Hands*, London, 1733 Vol. II, p. 86)

10 Medea contemplating the murder of her children

Black chalk

332×500 mm ($13\frac{1}{16} \times 19\frac{11}{16}$ ins.)

Verso: black chalk; two profiles directed to left – as for Medea on *recto*. Inscribed in pencil, at top of sheet '10' and in ink at foot 'No. 93'

PROVENANCE: B.V. 10

Again this is one of the 'sixteen studies' identified by John Romney as the immediate outcome of Romney's Italian visit (J.R. 257). The composition is related to others for the same subject in the sketch-book from the collection of the late Professor Isaacs (see cat. no. 9 above) – fol. 100v, 101, 101v, 102, 105v, 106v, 107, 107v, 108, 109v, 110, 110v, 111, 112, 113, 116 (unpaginated: folio references are those made by me at the time of the sale). The same sale contained a single mounted sheet (lot 15), also for the subject of Medea. A second sketch-book from the Isaacs collection (lot 14), almost entirely filled with sketches for portraits, contained a composition sketch for Medea and her children (fol. 22v). This sketch-book was dated on the front cover, 'May 1777'.

The subject is taken from *Medea* by Euripides. Medea, abandoned by Jason who has married Creon's daughter, is threatened with expulsion by Creon. Seeking revenge, she sends poisoned wedding garments to the new bride, and plans to murder her own two sons, the offspring of her liaison with Jason. Jason enters to try to save his sons from the wrath of Creon's house, but is just too late to save them from Medea. (*The Tragedies of Euripides*, translated by Dr Potter, London, 1781, Vol. I, pp. 240–312)

Romney's continued interest in the subject of Medea is witnessed by his later cartoon (*c.* 1777–80) and by the appearance of his name in the subscriber's list to Dr Potter's translation of *Euripides*, 1781. The cartoon given in 1823 to the Liverpool Royal Institution, is now in the Walker Art Gallery. The subject is the same, but the composition different. John Romney enthused about his father's treatment of the subject 'he could impart to the eye a language almost as impressive as that of the tongue, and communicate to the muscles and limbs all that appropriate action which they assume according to the impulse of different passions; he could represent with exact discrimination the shades by which kindred affections differ from each other, and even depict that agony of distress, when conflicting passions lacerate the

9

tenderest feelings of the heart – which is the highest effort of skill – the acme of pictorial expressions and his designs representing the struggle between disappointed love and maternal affection in the bosom of Medea, so beautifully described in the epigram on the picture painted by Timomachus, are convincing proofs of his ability in this respect' (J.R. 161).

It is interesting to note the extent to which Romney's treatment of the scene at this period of his life agrees with classical theory. The erudite John mentioned Timomachus, and it was the same painter who, with reference to Medea, occurred to Lessing: 'He did not paint Medea at the moment of her actually murdering her children, but just before, when motherly love is still struggling with jealousy. We anticipate the result and tremble at the idea of soon seeing Medea in the unmitigated ferocity, our imagination far outstripping anything the painter could have shown us at that terrible moment. For that reason he prolonged indecision, so far from displeasing us, makes us wish it had been continued in reality.' (Gotthold Ephraim Lessing: *Laocoon, an essay upon the limits of painting and poetry* translated by Ellen Frothingham, New York, The Noonday Press, 1957, p. 18.)

The dragons, which draw Medea's magic chariot, and bear her away from the scene of the slaughter, are already circling above the group in Romney's composition.

Having spent over two years in Italy, Romney returned home, again *via* France. He was back in London by 1 July 1775. In all probability he brought with him the large sketch-book already referred to (once in the collection of Sir Alfred Beit, subsequently that of the late Professor Isaacs of London; Sotheby's, 20 March 1963 lot 13, bought Folio Society. $11 \times 16\frac{1}{2}$ ins.). In the first months after his return to England he continued to work on the compositions which had occupied his attention in Rome. At the same time he must have begun to renew his old contacts, and to look for fresh commissions. Towards this end he leased a house in Cavendish Square, into which he moved at Christmas 1775. New sitters began to arrive at the attractive address: old sitters returned to him, because they appreciated his former work and rightly assumed that his skills could only be increased after such a prolonged Italian visit. Among these came Elizabeth Harriet Warren. She had been a child of about nine when Romney last painted her, in the famous group with her parents. Now she was seventeen. Romney painted the portrait of a beautiful débutante, as *Hebe*, the cup-bearer of the gods. Perhaps it was affection for the Warrens, as well as determination to make a great success of an important commission, that prompted him to sketch out the idea for his composition scores of times. It is instructive to look at a whole series of these sketches to see how generalised were the drawings he made for portraits.

11   Three portrait sketches

Pen with brown ink
291–349 × 483 mm ($11\frac{1}{2}$–$13\frac{3}{4}$ × 19 ins.)

Three slight sketches of a young woman standing. The central one appears to be the first idea for the portrait of Elizabeth Harriet Warren: the squiggle in her right hand denotes a wine jug, while the loops above her head to the left denote the eagle of his father Zeus.

12 Elizabeth Harriet Warren as Hebe, 1776

Pen with brown ink and brown wash
259×405 mm ($10\frac{3}{16} \times 15\frac{15}{16}$ ins.)
Recto: pen with brown ink and brown ink wash over pencil; *Dream of Atossa* – related to composition trials formerly in the Isaacs sketch-book (Sotheby's, 20 March 1963, lot 13)

PROVENANCE: L.D. 117, *verso*

Here the notion of dividing the composition in two down the middle, figure to the right and landscape to the left, is clearly tried out. The possibility of animating the figure by having her stepping down hill from right to left is also tested. Romney had already decided her hair should be blown out to the right, as that is indicated with the most rapid of scribbles.

13 Elizabeth Harriet Warren as Hebe, 1776

Pen with brown ink and brown wash
400×279 mm ($15\frac{3}{4} \times 11$ ins.)
Verso: pen with brown ink, possibly for *Catherine Vernon as Hebe* (see cat. no. 15 below)

PROVENANCE: L.D. 160

The movement from right to left is stressed.

14 Elizabeth Harriet Warren as Hebe, 1776

Brown watercolour wash over pencil
472×302 mm ($18\frac{9}{16} \times 11\frac{7}{8}$ ins.)
Small square of blue paper top left, inscribed '3'; beside that, in pencil, '24'
Verso: pencil; half reclining female figure $\frac{3}{4}$ facing left, leaning on left elbow to right

PROVENANCE: B.V. 24

This is listed by John Romney simply as 'Hebe' (J.R. 258). It is the most complete composition sketch which the Fitzwilliam Museum possesses for the portrait. It indicates clearly the eagle above, the landscape with waterfall at the left, and the elegant slender ewer carried by Miss Warren. The finished portrait, now entitled *Viscountess Bulkeley as Hebe* was shown in the Royal Academy Winter Exhibition, London 1955/6, no. 378 (colln. Sir Richard Williams-Bulkeley, Bart.). It was also celebrated in *British Art and the Mediterranean* by F. Saxl and R. Wittkower, 1948, repr. 63 (4). Romney's debt to his Italian visit is evident. On 26 April 1777 Elizabeth Harriet married Thomas James, 7th Viscount Bulkeley. Her portrait sittings had been in the previous year 1776, May 10, 14, 18, 21, December 21.

Small pen sketches, possibly for this figure, appear in a sketch-book in the Victoria and Albert Museum (19.C. 15/E. 4–1926) which also contains a detailed sketch of the ewer she carries (fol. 42 *verso*). This ewer is also shown in the hands of *Catherine Vernon as Hebe*, a portrait commissioned in 1777 by her brother-in-law, the Earl of Warwick (see cat. no. 15 below). There are many other sketches for Elizabeth Harriet Warren: National Gallery of Scotland, Ashmolean Museum, Oxford (Ruskin S.29); *ex* Haas Collection, Paris (No. 15 – sold Christie's, 12 July 1937, lot 20); and also *ex* Haas (No. 1072) Dilworth Collection, Yale University, New Haven, Conn. (Yale No. 378).

15   Catherine Vernon as Hebe, 1777

Pen with black ink over pencil
498 × 310 mm (19$\frac{5}{8}$ × 12$\frac{3}{16}$ ins.)
Verso: pencil; standing woman directed $\frac{3}{4}$ right, leaning on a column

PROVENANCE: L.D. 64

Catherine Vernon was second daughter and co-heiress of Richard Vernon, M.P. Her elder sister was married to the Earl of Warwick who commissioned this picture. Sittings: 1776 March 27; 1777 April 19, 22, 24, 29, May 5. The ewer she carries appears to be derived from a sketch made for Elizabeth Harriet Warren's ewer (see cat. no. 14 above). The Earl of Warwick's picture repr. W. & R.I, facing p. 45, as 'Miss Vernon as Hebe'.

16   Dream of Atossa, 1776

Pen with brown ink and brown ink wash over pencil
284–270 × 324 mm (11$\frac{3}{16}$–10$\frac{5}{8}$ × 12$\frac{3}{4}$ ins.)
Verso: inscribed in pencil, lower right, 'Aosa' (with long s)

PROVENANCE: L.D. 118

This sketch is directly related to L.D. 117 *recto* (see cat. no. 12 – L.D. 116 *verso* above), and can therefore be dated by association with the Elizabeth

Harriet Warren portrait drawing. The subject is another highly classical theme, typical of the years immediately succeeding Romney's Italian visit. A large charcoal cartoon on the same theme was among those presented by John Romney in 1823 to the Liverpool Royal Institution (now in the Walker Art Gallery, no. 18).

At the period when Romney was making drawings on this subject his friend the Rev. Robert Potter was translating the tragedies of Aeschylus. Romney painted Potter's portrait (W. & R. II, 125). We can imagine that their conversation turned on subjects in classical drama suitable for pictures. We know from notes in an Italian sketch-book (of which there are photographs in the Witt Library of the Courtauld Institute) that Greek drama had already been contemplated by him as a source (unpaginated: 'Subjects for Pictures —— / Ephagenia Sacrofising from / Euripides —— /'). Dr Potter may even have given Romney a draft translation of the passage detailing Atossa's dream, sending or bringing it at the time of his portrait sittings as he was later to send passages from Euripides (J.R. 159 & 160). Atossa's Dream occurs in *The Persians: The Tragedies of Aeschylus* translated by R. Potter (Norwich, 1777) pp. 470–1.

The present composition is not entirely convincing as Atossa's dream. However, both versions in the Fitzwilliam are so identified in an old hand. The cartoon in Liverpool is different. It relates to drawings in a sketch-book sold at Sotheby's 14 November 1962, lot 52 (fols. 17, 18, 18 *verso*, 32, 32 *verso*, 33, 33 *verso*, 34, 34 *verso*, 58 *verso*). The whereabouts of this sketch-book are unknown. Drawings related to the Fitzwilliam versions do not make the identification of subject any more secure (see sheet sold from the Haas collection, Christie's, 12 July 1937, part of lot 39, which links the present drawing with two others in the Fitzwilliam collection (L.D. 34 and L.D. 116) as the figure at the left holds a sword or staff above her head. In the Haas version there seem to be horses at the top right, where there are scribbles in the present drawing. There are two further versions of the composition, with horses at the top right, in a sketch-book belonging to a private collector in Pennsylvania. See also Folger Shakespeare Library, *Portfolio 9 verso*, where the composition is reversed. All that one can say of the subject with confidence is that it appears to be classical.

17 Sketch for portrait, presumably of young heiress

Pen with brown ink and brown ink wash over pencil
386 × 273 mm ($15\frac{3}{16}$ × $10\frac{3}{4}$ ins.)

PROVENANCE: L.D. 150

The classical flavour of Romney's work immediately after his return from Italy is exemplified not only in fancy subjects, but also in portraiture. Here we see a young girl apparently officiating at an altar. As in the portrait of

Elizabeth Harriet Warren, her hair is blown out to the right. Might this not signify 'fortune'? In Elizabeth Harriet Warren's case it certainly did. 'Fortune' is shown with her hair blown before because, if she is not grasped as she approaches, she is lost for ever. Alternatively, the motif may have been inspired by Raphael's *Galatea*.

18   Seated woman

Pen with brown ink and brown ink wash over pencil
286×215 mm ($11\frac{1}{4} \times 8\frac{7}{16}$ ins.)

PROVENANCE: L.D. 32

The pose, style of costume and high dressed hair relate this drawing to sheets of sketches from the Haas collection (Christie's 12 July 1937, part of lot 20; Smith 1962, Nos. 13 and 15). All these sheets measured approximately 197×162 mm. They would seem to have come from the same sketch-book kept by Romney 1776–7. This almost crouching pose – elbow on knee, and one hand supporting the head – was favoured by him immediately after his return from Italy, examples being *Lady Betty Hamilton* (the Countess of Derby) 1776–7, and *Mrs Birch*, 1777.

19   Sketch for the 'Dancing Gower children'

Light brown watercolour wash worked over with pen and brown ink, and brown ink wash
403×317 mm ($15\frac{7}{8} \times 12\frac{1}{2}$ ins.)

PROVENANCE: L.D. 58

REPRODUCED: Sutherland Gower (unnumbered plate at end of volume)

The charming scenes of May Day dancers which Romney described in Nice may have inspired his composition of the portrait of Lord Gower's children. The portrait, which was dated by John Romney 1776 (J.R. 141) must have been painted mostly in 1777. Details are given by W. & R. II, 63. The standing figure is Anne, daughter of the Earl's second wife; the little children, daughters of his third wife, are Charlotte Sophia, Georgiana and Susanna. Composition sketches probably belong to the early months of 1777. This one must have been made before 20 June that year, when the three year old Granville (not included here) is first noted in the appointments diary. In the final composition Lady Anne appears at the right, in the opposite sense to the present sketch; and Granville is introduced into the dancing ring behind the little girls.

20 King Lear Awake

Pen with brown ink and brown watercolour wash over traces of charcoal
337×459 mm (13¼×18 1/16 ins.)
Verso: pen with brown ink over chalk, the same composition in reverse.
This side was drawn first. From it parts of the *recto* have been traced. In
addition there are three small composition sketches at the top of the sheet.
Inscribed in pen with brown ink 'No. 108'

PROVENANCE: B.V. 8

If we possessed only such fair-copy versions of Romney's compositions,
we would miss the most powerful characteristics of his draughtsmanship, and
dating by style would be virtually impossible. This sheet is among the 'sixteen studies' identified by John Romney as the outcome of his father's
Italian visit. Apart from the classical counterpoise of the figures – the standing group compositionally springing from the point of the reclining figure's
feet (see also cat. no. 10 above), the sheet can be related to Romney's post
Italian period by the style of the *verso* (cf. cat. no. 24 below).

The subject is taken from *King Lear*, Act IV, sc. vii. Cordelia is brought
to the sleeping Lear by Kent and a doctor. Lear believes that he wakes in
heaven.

Romney's delight in the theatre and his love of Shakespeare were life long.
In his early years as a painter he produced not only *King Lear awakened by
his daughter Cordelia* (No. 1. in the 1762 Lottery at Kendal) but also *King
Lear in the tempest tearing off his robes* (No. 2 in the Lottery). We do not
now know what the Lear and Cordelia painting looked like. But the second
painting now hangs in the Mayor's Parlour at Kendal Town Hall. Comparison of that, with its rather crude figures small in proportion to the canvas,
gives us the measure of the advance Romney had made in fifteen years.

21 Lear Awakened by Cordelia

Pen with brown ink and brown wash over pencil
271×370 mm (10 11/16×14 9/16 ins.)
Verso: inscribed 'No. 105' in ink

PROVENANCE: B.V. 43

John Romney identifies this as 'Lear & Cordelia. Something in the style of
Guercino' (J.R. 259). It is comparable to two sheets in the Folger Shakespeare Library, both double sided, and bearing the same composition on
recto and *verso* (L.B.V. 41 and 42). The composition can be dated by association, as it occurs on the *verso* of a sheet showing *Psyche in Charon's Boat*
(see cat. no. 24 below). Another comparable composition trial occurs in the

1777–8 sketch-book in Hampstead Public Library (fol. 93 *recto*). For subject see cat. no. 20 above.

Dr Potter was not the only literary celebrity to sit to Romney in the years immediately succeeding the Italian visit, who became a friend for life. In 1776 Jeremiah Meyer, the miniaturist, introduced to Romney a poet who was giving up his house in London, and who wished to take with him to the country portraits of his best friends. From then on this William Hayley was to become the biggest single influence in Romney's life. Hayley was a poor poet, but a sociable and well-intentioned being. He was also filled with self satisfaction. An exaggerated belief in his own importance may have led him to over-emphasise his success in finding suitable subjects for Romney to depict. He may even have attempted to hook himself to Romney's obviously increasing fame. He became Romney's earliest biographer; and, as the artist was then already dead, he could weave himself happily into any fantasy he chose to depict. The first of these was the story of Cupid and Psyche. 'In the first years of my intimacy with Romney,' wrote Hayley, 'we formed many social projects of uniting poetry and design . . . we talked of producing a joint work on the adventures of Cupid and Psyche, from Apuleius. On this idea my friend drew no less than eight elegant cartoons in black chalk' (W.H. 78). The scheme never reached print. Hayley had abandoned his part of the project by 1777, in order to devote himself instead to the laudatory *Epistle to Romney* which was published in 1778 (W.H. 79). However Hayley's account is misleading: Romney had been working on the story of Cupid and Psyche long before he met Hayley. There are notes and drawings in Italian sketch-books, and Romney's work on the series continued long after Hayley had, by his own admission, cast the work aside. John Romney's account is nearer the truth: 'One of the earliest pictures Mr Romney painted after his return from Italy, was that of *Cupid and Psyche* most probably before he was established in Cavendish Square' (J.R. 143). One can only say that Hayley chimed in with, or latched on to Romney's interest of the moment. His most valuable contribution to the artist's work was that he offered for the next twenty years a long country summer holiday, annually. His first letter of invitation was written the first year of their acquaintance. It is florid, but sincere. It gives a taste of the hothouse nature of their association: 'I entreat you in the name of those immortal powers, the beautiful, and the sublime, whom you so ardently adore, or, to speak the language of your favourite Macbeth, "*I conjure you by that which you profess,*" to moderate your intense spirit of application, which preys so fatally on your frame – exchange, for a short time, the busy scenes and noxious air, of London, for the chearful tranquility and pure breezes of our Southern coast. – – – Here are three divinities, Health, Gaiety, and Friendship, that invite you very eagerly to this pleasant retreat, &c' (W.H. 73–5).

22 Psyche being rowed across the Styx

Pen with brown ink over traces of pencil, mostly erased
313×481 mm ($12\frac{5}{16} \times 18\frac{15}{16}$ ins.)

16

PROVENANCE: B.V. 38

REPRODUCED: Crookshank No. 7, p. 43

In January 1917 Charles Fairfax Murray presented to the Fitzwilliam a note-book which Romney had kept in Italy. It contains a few sketches, with several manuscript pages of notes on processes of painting, on pictures he had seen, and on subjects suitable for pictures. It is unpaginated; but on the seventh leaf from the front is a list headed, 'Passages for Picture in Poetry and History'. The fourth item is 'Psyche crossing the River Stickes'. In another sketch-book whose present location is unknown to me, but of which photographs exist in the Witt Library of the Courtauld Institute, there is a rapid composition sketch for the present drawing (this sketch-book contains mostly pencil drawings of statuary and paintings in Florence, and must have been used in late January 1775). It is impossible to say whether the present drawing was made in Italy at that time, or after Romney's return to England. He certainly worked on the Cupid and Psyche series extensively from 1776–7 or 1778. Hayley states that he made eight large cartoons in black chalk: seven of these are now in the Walker Art Gallery, having been given by John Romney to the Liverpool Royal Institution in 1823. A painting of *Cupid and Psyche* showing them in the final scene of the story, seated to-gether on a bed beyond which, through a gap in curtains, may be glimpsed the guests feasting at their wedding party, was given to Hayley's friend, the surgeon, Long. A ninth subject, unrepresented among the Liverpool car-toons, is the present one.

The story of Cupid and Psyche is told by an old nurse in the *Golden Ass* of Lucius Apuleius. Venus, annoyed by Cupid's love for Psyche, sets her seemingly impossible tasks. The fourth and last is to visit Proserpine and ask for some of her matchless beauty in a box, to repair the ravages wrought on Venus by the worry of Cupid's illness. The tower to which she goes to jump to her death advises her how to reach the Underworld in safety 'by and by thou shalt come unto a river of hell, whereas Charon is ferriman, who will first have his fare paid him, before he will carry the souls over the river in his boat, whereby you may see that avarice reigneth amongst the dead, neither Charon nor Pluto will do anything for nought' (*Golden Ass*, Book VI, chap. xxii, p. 114, translated by William Adlington, printed at the Ashendene Press, Chelsea, 1924).

Stylistically this may be compared to cat. nos. 8 and 9 above.

23 Psyche in Charon's Boat

Pen with brown ink
248×379 mm ($9\frac{3}{4} \times 14\frac{15}{16}$ ins.)
Verso: inscribed in ink 'No. 100'

PROVENANCE: B.V. 39

Psyche's instructions how to arrive in the Underworld (see cat. no. 22) continue 'And it shall come to pass as thou sittest in the boat thou shalt see an old man swimming on top of the river, holding up his deadly hands and desiring thee to receive him into the barke, but have no regard to his piteous cry.' (ibid, Book VI, chap. xxii, p. 114.) Identified by John Romney merely as 'from the fable of Cupid and Psyche' (J.R. 258).

24 Sketches for 'Apollo and Daphne' and for 'Psyche in Charon's Boat'

Pen with dark brown ink
254 × 390 mm (10 × 15 $\frac{3}{8}$ ins.)
Verso: pencil: *Lear awakened by Cordelia* (cf. cat. no. 21)

PROVENANCE: L.D. 113

Compare cat. nos. 22 and 23 above.

Romney's first ideas for the arrangement of figures in a composition were often slight. Rather than alter details in a figure, he evidently preferred to redraw the whole.

25 Thetis

Pen with brown ink and brown ink wash over very slight pencil
257 × 383 mm (10 $\frac{1}{8}$ × 15 $\frac{1}{16}$ ins.)

PROVENANCE: L.D. 85

The identification is that of John Romney for B.V. 19 & 21, *Thetis comforting Achilles* (J.R. 258). There are further versions of the figure in a sketchbook in the Victoria and Albert Museum (19 C 15 – E. 4–1926). It should be dated 1776/7, see fols. 13 *verso*, 14, 15 *verso*, 17, 18, 19, 25 *verso*, 26, 31 *verso*, 32, 38 *verso*. Compositionally B.V. 19 comes between the versions in the sketch-book and the present drawing.

26 Head of Saul

Black chalk partly worked with stump
438 × 311 mm (17 $\frac{1}{4}$ × 12 $\frac{1}{4}$ ins.)
Verso: black chalk, standing woman, $\frac{3}{4}$ face to left, right arm across breast, leans on table

PROVENANCE: B.V. 46

REPRODUCED: Sutherland Gower, end plate, incorrectly as 'belonging to Herbert Thring, Esq.'

The head study for *David playing before Saul* (see B.V. 47) is typical of Romney's work in black chalk of the period 1776–7, when he was making large cartoons in black chalk such as those presented to the Liverpool Royal Institution (see cat. no. 22).

27   Odin before the Prophetess

Pen with grey ink and pale brown watercolour wash over pencil
271×218 mm ($10\frac{11}{16} \times 8\frac{9}{16}$ ins.)
Verso: pencil, *The Waking of Psyche*, sketch for the large black chalk cartoon now in the Walker Art Gallery Liverpool, having been given by John Romney to the Liverpool Royal Institution in 1823

PROVENANCE: B.V. 55

EXHIBITED: *La peinture romantique anglaise et les préraphaélites*, Paris, Petit Palais, Janvier–Avril, 1972, no. 218.

Like the sketch on the *verso*, *The Descent of Odin* was one of the subjects of a large black chalk cartoon presented by John Romney to the Liverpool Royal Institution in 1823 (no. 12 – see J.R. 267). The majority of these cartoons appear to have been made in the years 1776–7. John Romney identifies the subject as 'From Grey's Descent of Odin' (J.R. 259). *The Descent of Odin* was first included among Grey's collected poems in 1768 (London *bis*; Glasgow; Dublin; Cork). Odin rides on his coal black steed to the Gates of Hell to ask the prophetess his fate.

There is also a pencil sketch for this subject in the Fitzwilliam – M.D. 28.

28   Mater Dolorosa

Pen with brown ink over pencil
507×308 mm ($19\frac{15}{16} \times 12\frac{1}{8}$ ins.)
Verso: pencil; seated woman $\frac{3}{4}$ to right, hands clasped and raised before her

PROVENANCE: L.D. 121

The first commission received by Romney after his return from Italy, other than for a portrait, came from Thomas Orde (later Orde-Powlett, first Lord Bolton). Orde had come up to Cambridge from Eton in 1765 when he was seventeen. In 1768 he was made a Fellow of King's College. He may have met Romney in Italy; for at the time of Romney's return to London they appear to have been personal friends. From all accounts he gave Romney the commission for a religious painting in 1776, the year before he sat for his own portrait. John Romney outlines what happened: Thomas Orde, 'influenced by that grateful feeling and pious regard, which every liberal minded man must entertain for the place of his education, had intended to have presented to the Society of King's College, Cambridge, of which he had recently been a fellow, an Altar-piece for their admirable chapel, a structure in every part perfect except in the decorations of the Altar, which seemed to require some picture of a solemn but splendid effect. – The idea which Mr Orde had suggested, was a *Mater Dolorosa*, or what the Italians call *Maria alla Croce*. The picture was in a state of great forwardness, but in consequence of his disappointment, it was never afterwards touched; and Mr Romney lost both his hundred guineas and his time, which latter was to him at that period far the greater loss of the two' (J.R. 136–7). The occasion for the disappointment was that the Earl of Carlisle presented the College with an 'old master' – a *Deposition* then supposed to be by Daniele da Volterra, but now identified as by Siciolante da Sermoneta.

The only studies known for the King's College altar piece advance no further than pen and wash drawings. John Romney gave four to the Fitzwilliam collection (B.V. 47, 48, 49 and 50 – see cat. no. 29). In Christie's 1807 sale lot 87 was 'Religion, ditto (i.e. "a large study"), designed for King's College Chapel, Cambridge': all the items in that sale not designated as cartoons were presumably in oils.

In the Fitzwilliam collection see also M.D. 65. Other studies are in the Folger Shakespeare Library – (L.B.V. 58, and 59). None are very convincing as religious works. The present pen study is directly related to B.V. 49, which was probably traced through from it, and then elaborated with black chalk and stump as cat. no. 29.

29   Head study for 'Mater Dolorosa'

Charcoal worked with stump over slight pencil, strengthened with black chalk
497 × 314 mm ($19\frac{9}{16}$ × $12\frac{3}{8}$ ins.)

PROVENANCE: B.V. 50

See notes on cat. no. 28. Given this commission for a genre with which he was unfamiliar and for which he had apparently little natural feeling, Romney turned to an Italian prototype: this head study is very similar to that of Mary in Titian's *Assumption of the Virgin* which Romney had studied in the Academia, Venice, in 1775. He uses the same technique as he did for the large cartoons and for the *Head of Saul* (see cat. no. 26).

30 Gil Morrice

Pen with grey ink and grey watercolour wash over pencil, partly erased
381 × 571 mm (15 × 22½ ins.)
Verso: inscribed in ink 'No. 73'

PROVENANCE: B.V. 103

The subject, for which I know no preliminary drawings, is identified by John
Romney 'Gil Morrice: from Percy's Reliques of ancient English Poetry'
(J.R. 264). Stylistically, and as a subject from English poetry, it should be
associated with *Odin before the Prophetess* (cat. no. 27). Percy's *Reliques* was
first published in 1765. In the ballad, Gil (or 'Child') Morrice, the natural
child of the Baron's Lady, is suspected of being his mother's lover. Lord
Bernard, her husband, having intercepted a letter appointing an assignation,
goes out to the rendez-vous in the woods, and kills him. (Percy's *Reliques*,
3rd edn, London, Dodsley, 1775, vol. III, p. 95.) The medium suggests work
for engraved illustration. Romney's later projected illustrations for Hayley's
works, *The Triumphs of Temper*, and *Essay on old Maids* (see cat. nos. 73 and
74) were also in grey wash.

31 Agitated crowd

Brown ink wash over pencil
343 × 543 mm (13½ × 21⅜ ins.)

PROVENANCE: L.D. 165

The date of this drawing is uncertain, but the long robes suggest a classical
subject. It probably belongs to the period after Romney's return from Italy.
Later scenes of distress and devastation are enclosed in heavily hatched dark-
ness (see cat. nos. 113 to end).

32 Scene of a massacre

Pen with brown ink and brown ink wash
241 × 443 mm (9½ × 17 7/16 ins.)
Verso: inscribed in pencil lower right 'A'; in pencil at centre '43'

PROVENANCE: L.D. 172

Possibly a composition sketch for the *Destruction of the children of Niobe*.
Romney made elaborate notes on the Niobe group in the sketch-book which
he kept in Florence in late January 1775 (see cat. no. 22). Romney made
several large drawings of the subject, one of which his son included in his gift

21

to Cambridge (B.V. 13). The disposition of Niobe and her children is in a rough triangle, as here: but the similarities are only of the most general nature. The drawing style and the composition indicate a date during or soon after his Italian visit. The figures are grouped together and interact, completely independent of their context. The composition is neo-classical.

33 Iphigenia asleep with her maidens

Brown wash over pencil
328 × 568 mm ($12\frac{15}{16}$ × $22\frac{3}{8}$ ins.)
Verso: pencil, another version of the same group

PROVENANCE: L.D. 163

This drawing shows the incredibly rapid 'short-hand' style of notation used by Romney to work out a composition. A more finished version of the subject, but with the three figures reversed, was lent to the 1962 Smith College exhibition (no. 43). Another version of the same subject was on the London art market in 1972. The subject is from Boccaccio's *Decameron*, and occurs in the first story told by Pamfilo on the fifth day. Cimon, the handsome but simple son of a grand Cypriot gentleman, is banished to the country by his father. Living like a shepherd he one day sees the beautiful Iphigenia, scantily clothed, sleeping with her maidens by a pool. Her beauty transforms him. He returns to the city and makes good as a gentleman and scholar: after various trials he is eventually united with Iphigenia. The more elaborate version of the composition agree with Boccaccio in so many details that there can be no doubt of the identification: the setting is 'a fair coppice – which was then all in leaf'. The central figure is 'a very fair damsel asleep upon the grass, with so thin a garment upon her body that it hid well nigh nothing of her snowy flesh. She was covered only from the waist down with a very white and light coverlet; and at her feet slept on likewise two women.' Finally there is the outline of the amazed rustic peering over the hedge: 'When Cimon espied the young lady he halted and leaning upon his staff fell, without saying a word, to gazing most intently upon her with the utmost admiration.'

The present drawing is for the sleeping women – obviously the chief attraction of the subject. Rubens, too, as Romney probably knew, had chosen it for the same reason (*Cimon and Iphigeneia*, Kunsthistorisches Museum, Vienna). The chance to depict languorous female nudes prompted Romney to take a subject from Boccaccio. If he took other subjects from this author, they have not been identified: but, since the *Decameron* offers a wealth of subjects of that innocent licentiousness so much appreciated in the mid-eighteenth century, it is likely that he did so. It is impossible to tell how far John Romney's censorship of his father's works went.

34 Arcadian Lovers

Pen with brown ink and brown ink wash over pencil
286 × 289 mm ($11\frac{1}{4} \times 11\frac{3}{8}$ ins.)
Verso: inscribed in pencil '15' and 'Orpheus'

PROVENANCE: L.D. 94

As the young man holds a lyre it seems likely that these figures represent Orpheus and Eurydice. John Romney, who included another such subject (B.V. 31) in his gift to Cambridge, called it 'Damon and Musidora from Thomson's Seasons' (J.R. 258): but, as that story is of two coy lovers who adored each other secretly without revealing their passion, the identification seems doubtful. We know that John Romney's knowledge of the subject of Orpheus and Eurydice was shaky; he identified a preliminary sketch (B.V. 37) for the Liverpool cartoon 'Eurydice fleeing from Aristaeus' as 'Psyche' (J.R. 258). That his confusion was real is born out by the fact that he believed he had given two, rather than three, cartoons of Orpheus and Eurydice to Liverpool (J.R. 172). Both in the present composition and in B.V. 31 the girl appears to gaze deep into the young man's eyes.

35 Gladiator on horseback

Pen with brown ink and brown wash over pencil
317 × 368 mm ($12\frac{1}{2} \times 14\frac{1}{4}$ ins.)

PROVENANCE: With Agnew's; R. E. Balfour, Esq., Fellow of King's College, Cambridge; bequeathed by him, 1945 (No. 2733)

Two comparable studies are in the Witt Collection, but the exact subject has not been identified.

36 Two standing women

Pen with brown ink and brown ink wash over pencil
316 × 218 mm ($12\frac{7}{16} \times 8\frac{9}{16}$ ins.)
Verso: inscribed in pencil at centre '16'

PROVENANCE: L.D. 159

This may have been a sketch for a portrait. Romney often painted sisters in close relation to each other – e.g. the so-called *Daughters of Lord Malmesbury* (repr. Sutherland Gower end plate – presumably the *Sisters of Lord Malmesbury*, being the Misses Harris) painted in 1777. Except in the case of mothers and children, Romney's compositional invention for double portraits was less fertile than that of Sir Joshua Reynolds.

37 Family Group

Pen with brown ink and brown ink wash over pencil
276×245–280 mm (10⅞×9⅝–11 ins.)

PROVENANCE: L.D. 139

This simian composition may be a family group, but it could equally well be two women with a child upon their knees, or simply two women embracing. It was the balance of the composition and not the precise delineation which interested Romney at this stage of a work's evolution. Such drawings are obviously private jottings, and were not for public display. They have a frank power of expression which appeals to the twentieth century.

38 Two crouching women

Pen with dark brown ink and ink wash over pencil
300–295×224 mm (11$\frac{13}{16}$–11⅝×8$\frac{13}{16}$ ins.)

PROVENANCE: L.D. 185

As already noted, Romney quite often used crouching poses for ladies' portraits in 1777 (see cat. no. 18). The present drawing, a curious composition for a portrait, is more likely to be a trial of a subject of two women mourning at a grave, or officiating at an altar. Nevertheless it is probably a work of the late 1770s.

39 'The Weird Sisters'

Pen with brown ink and brown ink wash over pencil
304×484 mm (12×19⅛ ins.)
Inscribed, top left corner on a square of blue paper '2'; in pencil (erased) '52'
Verso: in ink 'No. 151'

PROVENANCE: B.V. 52

If the title given by John Romney (J.R. 259) is correct, the subject is from *Macbeth*, Act I, sc. iii. Macbeth and Banquo meet the three witches on the heath near Forres. Romney repeated the subject several times: the three crouching hags pointing to the right recur in drawings in the Folger Shakespeare Library (L.B.V. 52 and 54). There is also another sheet in the Fitzwilliam which shows three hags directed to the right (L.D. 78), but in a rather different composition. On the *verso* of that drawing is inscribed in pencil 'L. Witch', a subject we know that Romney worked on (W.H. 83).

The theatre, and particularly the plays of Shakespeare, held enormous fascination for Romney. At the outset of his career he painted subjects from *Lear*. Throughout his life the animation of the theatre was to fire his visual imagination, particularly when he was drawing incidents from a drama. For instance, in the Folger sketch-book inscribed 'Macbeth/Midsummernight dream/McBeth', there is a series of sketches for the Banquet scene in which, as we turn the pages, we see the reactions of the guests to the appearance of the ghost in almost cinematographic progression. This is also true in other sketch-books, and for other subjects, where the same scene is jotted down on consecutive pages. When a sketch-book is broken up, we lose this effect for ever.

Refuelling his imagination, Romney went frequently to the theatre. As he understood little or no Italian, he must have been glad to return to the English speaking theatre after his Italian visit. He appears to have cared little about the discomforts of queuing outside a theatre, even if he got soaked in the process. John Romney tells such a tale: 'In the beginning of the summer of this year (1776) he was seized with a severe disorder which had nearly proved fatal. Garrick had promised to sit to him for his portrait; . . . On the 10th June, when that great actor made his final appearance upon the stage, Mr Romney, along with the multitude, was attracted to the doors of Drury Lane theatre; partly, like others, by simple curiosity; but more especially with a view to avail himself of that opportunity, in order to study with great advantage the features of his intended sitter. His endeavours to gain an entrance were, however, ineffectual, and he consoled himself for the disappointment by repairing to the other theatre. Unluckily, while he was standing in the crowd, a slight shower chanced to fall, not such as to induce him to return home; but sufficient to communicate so much dampness to his dress, as to become afterwards the cause of his catching cold when heated in the theatre. Mr Cumberland happening to call just at the time, and finding him in a most dangerous state, and under the defective advice of an apothecary, immediately sent for Sir Richard Jebb, who, as soon as he saw his patient, instantly ordered him to drink a bottle of Madeira. He afterwards told Mr Cumberland that Mr Romney's life could not have been saved, if advice had been delayed half an hour longer!' (J.R. 137).

The Garrick portrait was never painted: but Romney's experience in depicting another famous actor of the day, John Henderson, was happier. Food, drink and conviviality combined to foster a friendship which appears to have been entirely genial, and to have given Romney the chance of producing some splendid portrait sketches. John Henderson (1747–85), the son of an Irish pastor, had been intended for a career as draughtsman and silversmith: but at the age of 21 he determined to abandon that profession for the stage. Garrick said that he showed no promise, and refused to take him on. However, he introduced him to Palmer the manager of the Bath company. There Henderson was such a resounding success that in 1777 Coleman, who had taken on a little theatre in the Haymarket, engaged him and brought him to London as Shylock: this was followed by Lear, Richard III, Don John and two Falstaffs. He was so brilliant that Sheridan engaged him for Drury Lane. Garrick had by this time retired (see

Brander Matthews and Laurence Hutton, *Actors and Actresses of Great Britain and the United States, from the days of David Garrick to the present time*, vol. I, New York, 1886, pp. 253–67).

At about the time of Henderson's arrival in London Romney joined with some friends in forming a small private literary and dining club; known eventually as the 'Unincreasables'. It had a limit of eight members, among whom were the elder Sheridan, Henderson, Romney, Evans the bookseller, the Rev. Charles Este and Long the surgeon. Romney had the opportunity to draw Henderson off stage as well as on.

40   Henderson as Macbeth

Pencil
336·5 × 393·5 mm (13¼ × 15½ ins.)
Verso: pencil; sketch for the same, but including Banquo at left and witches at right

PROVENANCE: L.D. 115

Henderson sat to Romney in 1780: October 13, 18, 24, 29 and December 23. Although his greatest successes were in comic roles, Macbeth was probably chosen as being more dignified for a portrait than Falstaff. In the painting Henderson is bare headed and clasps a naked sword, close to the hilt under his bare arm. On this sheet Romney seems to be experimenting not only with the hat, but with the draping of the plaid about the actor's shoulders.

41   Three Witches for 'Henderson as Macbeth'

Pencil
202·5 × 130 mm (8 × 5⅛ ins.)

PROVENANCE: M.D. 27

REPRODUCED: Crookshank, p. 43, plate 14

See cat. no. 40. John Romney notes 'This picture was painted about the time when Sheridan and Henderson had their public readings ... Mr Romney being present at one of those recitations, was so forcibly struck with the countenance of a man staring with all his attention at Sheridan, that he could not refrain from studying it carefully as an appropriate representation of a witch's face; and having on his return home sketched it on canvas, he afterwards introduced it into the picture of Henderson.' (J.R. 166–7.) Matthews, *Gallery of Theatrical Portraits*, states that the other witches are portraits of Charles Macklin and John Williams. The witches were to the right of the canvas, as we know from a mezzotint of the portrait engraved by John Jones and published in 1787. There is also a small oil sketch in the Folger Shakespeare Library, Washington D.C., U.S.A. which shows the whole of the original composition. The actual portrait has been cut down since it was engraved; and it now excludes the witches.

42 Falstaff in the Boar's Head Tavern

Pencil
394 × 537–540 mm (15½ × 21⅛–21¼ ins.)
Verso: inscribed in ink '144' (cancelled)

PROVENANCE: B.V. 128

Identified by John Romney as 'King Henry IV Act 2 scene iv' (J.R. 265), this must be from Part II of Shakespeare's play. Falstaff consorts with the hostess and Doll Tearsheet in the Boar's Head Tavern, Eastcheap; and there he is joined by Bardolph, who raises Mistress Dorothy's anger. The main character is obviously played by Henderson, whose best parts were judged by the playwright Richard Cumberland to be Shylock, Sir Giles Overreach and Falstaff. Of Henderson as Falstaff, John Romney says, 'Henderson was a most accomplished actor, and had a fine turn of humour; but his person had defects which no art could conceal. In Falstaff, in which those defects did not appear, or, perhaps, rather aided the character, he was pre-eminent; he wanted, however, expression and his features were too round.' (J.R. 166.) See cat. nos. 43 and 47b for similar head studies.

43 Henderson: study for head of Falstaff

Pencil
139 × 162 mm (5½ × 6⅜ ins.)

PROVENANCE: M.D. 67

Portrait sketch of John Henderson the actor; possibly a trimmed fragment from a sketch-book. This study is for *Falstaff in the Boar's Head Tavern* (see cat. no. 42).

44 Falstaff and the Merry Wives of Windsor

Pencil
375 × 416 mm (14¹⁵⁄₁₆ × 16⅜ ins.)
Verso: inscribed in pencil 'After 25'

PROVENANCE: L.D. 127

Probably a scene from *The Merry Wives of Windsor*: Mistress Ford and Mistress Page hustle the reluctant Falstaff into hiding as their husbands return. Only the head of Falstaff if clearly defined, a portrait sketch of the actor John Henderson. In the Dilworth Collection, Yale University Art Gallery, there is another version of Falstaff hustled along by the two women (see Smith College, 1962, No. 33, *repr.*).

45   Falstaff with the body of Hotspur

Pen with black ink and grey watercolour wash over traces of pencil
343 × 560–557 mm (13$\frac{1}{2}$ × 22$\frac{1}{16}$–21$\frac{15}{16}$ ins.)
Verso: inscribed in ink 'No. 53'

PROVENANCE: B.V. 129

The incident occurs in *Henry IV*, Part I, act V, sc. iv. Prince Hal kills Henry Percy (Hotspur). Falstaff, to avoid the dangers of battle is lying nearby, shamming dead. When the Prince has moved on Falstaff rises to stab Hotspur in the thigh. He begins to bear the body off, intending to claim that he has slain him. Falstaff is, of course, played by John Henderson. See cat. nos. 47a, 47b and 47c for similar head studies.

46   Falstaff relinquishing the body of Hotspur

Pen with black ink and grey watercolour wash over traces of pencil
391–384 × 511–517 mm (15$\frac{3}{8}$–15$\frac{1}{8}$ × 20$\frac{1}{8}$–20$\frac{3}{8}$ ins.)
Verso: inscribed in ink 'No. 50'

PROVENANCE: B.V. 130

REPRODUCED: Sutherland Gower, end plate, as 'Falstaff'

This incident in *Henry IV*, Part I, act V, sc. iv, immediately succeeds that depicted in cat. no. 45 above. Falstaff, startled at the sudden return of Prince Hal, relinquishes the body of Hotspur (killed by Prince Hal) whom he was himself about to claim to have killed. Again Falstaff is played by John Henderson. See cat. nos. 47a, 47c and 47d which may be studies for Falstaff's head.

47a, b, c & d   Portrait studies of John Henderson as Falstaff

Pencil
47a   90 × 93 mm (3$\frac{9}{16}$ × 3$\frac{11}{16}$ ins.)
47b   67 × 86 mm (2$\frac{5}{8}$ × 3$\frac{3}{8}$ ins.)
47c   65 × 86 mm (2$\frac{9}{16}$ × 3$\frac{3}{8}$ ins.)
47d   89 × 95 mm (3$\frac{1}{2}$ × 3$\frac{3}{4}$ ins.)

PROVENANCE: M.D. 66a, b, c and d

All appear to be trimmed fragments, possibly from a sketch-book, and are mounted together on one board. All are portrait sketches, evidently from the life, of Romney's friend the actor, John Henderson. Cat. nos. 47a, 47c and 47d may have been used for the finished drawings *Falstaff with the body of Hotspur* (cat. no. 45) and *Falstaff relinquishing the body of Hotspur* (cat. no. 46). Cat. no. 47b may have been used for *Falstaff in the Boar's Head Tavern* (cat. no. 42). In the Folger Shakespeare Library, there is a comparable sheet of studies evidently for the mouth of Henderson as Falstaff.

48 Portrait composition *c.* 1780

Pencil with dark brown ink over heavy pencil
514×317 mm ($20\frac{1}{4} \times 12\frac{1}{2}$ ins.)

PROVENANCE: L.D. 59

This sketch for a portrait shows what care Romney took not only in the positioning of the figure, but also in such details as the sculptured motif on the plinth on which she leans. The hair style, not dressed high as in the 1770s, but rather bouffant and bound with ribbon, is typical of the early 1780s. The pose precisely reverses that of Mrs Maxwell (see Chamberlain, facing p. 274 and W. & R. I, facing p. 94), whose sittings began in the early summer of 1780.

49 Aeneas before the Cumaean Sibyl

Pen with dark brown ink and brown ink wash over pencil
214×275 mm ($8\frac{7}{16} \times 10\frac{13}{16}$ ins.)
Verso: pencil; sketch for the same, save that crowd now appears to right of the priestess and warrior

PROVENANCE: L.D. 83

The identification of subject is tentative, but not without foundation. In the John Romney Gift there are two large drawings (B.V. 14 and B.V. 15) probably made in Italy, which are identified as 'the Cumaean Sibyl foretelling to Aeneas his future destiny' (J.R. 258). The subject is confirmed in Romney's own hand: the notebook presented to the Fitzwilliam Museum by Charles Fairfax Murray in 1917 contains a page already noted under cat. no. 22 above, after the Psyche entry the fifth subject is 'Eaneas (sic) with the Cumean Cybel (sic)'. On Romney's return to England his renewed interest in the theatre may have suggested a more dramatic rendering of the same subject. A version of the present composition occurred in sketch-book Truro

No. 1. On internal evidence this sketch-book should be dated 1782–3. The sketch-book was paginated and the composition of warrior, priestess and crowd occurred on p. 41.

50 Scene of Supplication

Pen with brown ink, and brown ink wash over pencil
265 × 206 mm ($10\frac{7}{16}$ × $8\frac{1}{8}$ ins.)
Verso: pencil; loose scribbles – part of a much larger composition sketch

PROVENANCE: L.D. 168

The subject is unidentified, but the style places the drawing in the early 1780s (see Truro No. 1, location now unknown).

Apart from high drama, both theatrical and classical, Romney was interested in the problems of depicting scenes from contemporary life. During his apprenticeship, or soon after, he had painted *A Quarrel*, *A Droll Scene in an ale-house* and *A Tooth Drawing by Candle-light*, all of which appeared in the 1762 Kendal Lottery (J.R. 24–5). Concentration on building up his practice as a portrait painter, and on acquiring a knowledge of subjects in classical and modern literature suitable for history pictures, may have diverted him for several years from topics in contemporary life. But he kept his eye on 'Nature'. In the Italian notebook, given to the Fitzwilliam by Charles Fairfax Murray in 1917, he jotted down some 'Observations – Make the Simplicity of Nature your standard – Beware that your fancy do not carry you beyond your good sence. Let every thing be filled with the latter – Nature is the fountane that over flows with examples of it.

Is it not a convincing proof that exaggeration of passion is a fault when in nature the endevouring to conceel them affect you and the exagerating them disgust you.

Allways try your compositions by the scale of common sence.' (fol. 3)

After Romney's return to England his reflections on contemporary life suggested satirical interpretations. In the sketch-book kept in 1776–7 now in the Victoria and Albert Museum (19 C 15 E. 4–1926) there is the draft of a letter. 'I should like you to write a satire on the time marking the follies peculiar to this age and to draw the conspicuous charracters of folly full length and to work up a system of that sort that would mark this age. I do not know any subject equal to it for copiousness variety and entertainment beneficialness to mankind. There is religious pretension, fashions and tastes that prevail at this time and to oppose this the grett light that is thrown on all the sciences, the extraordinary industry of men in that line and our superiority to all nations, or purity of love and superiority in all arts we pursue.' (Fol. 1, *recto* and *verso*) The intended recipient of the letter is not indicated.

His barely literate scrawls cannot have helped to clarify his thoughts very effectively, even to himself; but, as we shall see, the idea of a satire on modern life was not irrelevant to some of the subjects he was to draw.

51 'Hume in some domestic scene'

Pen with brown ink, grey watercolour wash and traces of pencil
314×451 mm (12⅜×17¾ ins.)
Verso: inscribed in ink 'No. 65'

PROVENANCE: B.V. 87

John Romney comments: 'As far as I remember Mr Romney said this subject
represented Hume in some domestic scene' (J.R. 261). Romney shows the
participants in contemporary dress. The strength of the work is in their
expressive heads. There are few clues as to the source of the subject: the
startled visitor seems to be staring at a crucifix hung above the sick man's
head. It could be the discovery of a Scottish Catholic on his death bed. The
1745 uprising had come when Romney had been an impressionable ten year
old; and the feelings of Protestants about Catholics were very sensitive
throughout his lifetime. Remember that Hume was a Scot and a rationalist
philosopher to whom the outward trappings of religion, especially of the
Catholic persuasion, were mumbo-jumbo. This could be an illustration by
Romney of that 'religious pretention' which he suggested should be satir-
ized.

The drawing is in a medium associated with the preparation of a composition for illustrative print making.

52 The Wronged Maid: the dissecting room

Pen with dark brown ink and grey wash over pencil
319×508 mm (12⁹⁄₁₆×20 ins.)
Verso: inscribed in ink 'No. 69'

PROVENANCE: B.V. 101

John Romney not only identifies the subject of this and the following drawing but transcribes the story from a manuscript 'found among Mr Romney's
papers . . . About seventeen years ago a young woman from the country, of
a very agreeable person, was servant to a man, who had all the vices attendant
on the corruption of large cities. Struck with her charms, he tried all methods
of seduction. She was virtuous, she resisted. Her discretion only inflamed the
passion of her master, who, not being able to prevail with her, devised the
blackest and most abominable revenge. He clandestinely put into her box,
where she kept her clothes, several things belonging to himself, and marked
with his own name; he then exclaimed he was robbed, sent for a constable
and made his deposition. When the box was opened, the effects which he
claimed, were known. The poor girl, being imprisoned, had only tears for
her defence, and all that she said in answer to the interrogatories, was, that

she was innocent. Our criminal jurisprudence cannot be sufficiently condemned, when we consider that the judges had no suspicion of the wickedness of the accuser, and that they enforced the law in its utmost rigour; a rigour that is extreme, and which ought to be banished from our code, and give place to a simple chastisement, which would leave fewer robberies unpunished.

'Innocent as she was, she was condemned to be hanged. She was unskilfully executed, it being the first essay of the executioner's son. A surgeon bought the body. As he was preparing that evening to dissect it, he perceived some remains of warmth; the knife drop from his hands, and he put into his bed her whom he was going to anatomize.

'His endeavour to restore her to life succeeded; at the same time he sent for an ecclesiastic, with whose discretion and experience he was well acquainted; as well to consult him on this strange event, as to make him a witness of his conduct. At the moment when the unfortunate girl opened her eyes she thought herself in the other world, and seeing the figure of the priest, who had a large head, and features strongly marked, (for I knew him, and from him had this account), she clasped her hands with terror, and exclaimed, *Eternal Father, you know my innocence, have mercy on me*! She did not cease to invoke the ecclesiastic, thinking she saw God himself. It was long before she could be convinced that she was not dead, so strongly the idea of punishment and death had impressed her imagination. Nothing could be more affecting, or more expressive, than this exclamation of an innocent soul, to him whom she considered as her supreme Judge; and without her endearing beauty, this sight alone was sufficient to interest strongly a man of sensibility and observation. What a picture for a painter! What a narration for a philosopher! What a lesson for a lawyer!' (J.R. 262–3).

This tale from contemporary life could, like cat. no. 51, take its place in that 'satire on the time marking the follies peculiar to this age' which we saw Romney urging upon some friend in the late 1770s.

Once more the medium is that associated with preparation for print making.

53 The Wronged Maid: her awakening

Pen with brown ink and grey watercolour wash over pencil
315 × 506 mm (12$\frac{7}{16}$ × 19$\frac{15}{16}$ ins.)

PROVENANCE: B.V. 102

See cat. no. 52. The identification is by John Romney. Again the drawing is worked in a medium associated with preparation for print making. However, unlike cat. no. 51, the characters involved are not shown in contemporary dress.

54 Wealth and Poverty

Pen with brown ink and grey watercolour wash over black chalk
381–387 × 317 mm (15–15$\frac{1}{4}$ × 12$\frac{1}{2}$ ins.)
Verso: inscribed in ink 'No. 80'

PROVENANCE: B.V. 114

The second of two versions of this subject in the John Romney Gift. The identification of subject given in the manuscript catalogue to his Gift is rather fuller than the printed version. 'These two Sketches seen to be studies from nature. It is probable that Mr R. saw in his walks an interesting Girl in the character of a Street-sweeper; asking charity; with whose manner & expression he was so forcibly struck as to commit the idea to paper. Immediately on his return home.

It is only by studying nature, unsophisticated nature, that an Artist can expect to attain to excellence' (MS Catalogue, Fitzwilliam Museum, Cambridge).

However, the drawing seems to be more than a random note from life, for there are several studies for similar compositions (Fitzwilliam Museum B.V. 113 and B.V. 114; L.D. 92 and L.D. 93 – see cat. no. 55). There were also studies for the composition in the collection of the late Professor Isaacs. Moreover Romney tried out various effects, especially depicting the figure of 'Wealth' in a variety of ways, and showing 'Poverty' not only as a street sweeper, but also as a beggar carrying a small child (L.D. 92). This might well be another illustration of 'follies peculiar to this age'. Again the medium is that associated with preparation for print making.

55 Wealth – for 'Wealth and Poverty'

Pencil
372 × 256–260 mm (14$\frac{5}{8}$ × 10$\frac{1}{16}$–10$\frac{1}{4}$ ins.)
Verso: pencil, very slight composition scribble, possibly of a child being suckled by a wolf. Old inscriptions, pencil, '27' and 'a'

PROVENANCE: L.D. 93

The satirical effect of the whole composition (see cat. no. 54) would have been greater had the figure of Wealth indeed been so depicted. However, Romney's determination to avoid exaggeration presumably made him settle on a more conventional, less bloated young lady to play the rôle.

56 A Mother instructing her child

Pen with brown ink and brown ink wash over pencil
502 × 311 mm (19$\frac{3}{4}$ × 12$\frac{1}{4}$ ins.)
Verso: inscribed in ink 'No. 58'

The title is that given by John Romney. This drawing is likely to be a sketch for a portrait, but the identification has yet to be made.

57   A Woman caressing a lap dog

Pen with brown ink and brown watercolour wash over traces of pencil (mostly erased)
456×313 mm ($17\frac{15}{16} \times 12\frac{5}{16}$ ins.)

PROVENANCE: B.V. 23

The identification is John Romney's. His father painted women holding dogs on several occasions. The famous portrait of Emma Hart as 'Nature' (now in the Frick Collection, New York) shows her with a small spaniel in her arms. Ward and Roberts list other portraits of ladies with dogs: *Miss Popham* (with a King Charles spaniel) *c.* 1772; *the Hon. Miss Stanley* (with a spaniel), 1777; *Lady Louisa Lennox* (with spaniel), 1777; *Miss Holbech* (with long-haired Scotch terrier), 1781 – when the lady was 4 years old; *Mrs Moody* 1786; and *Henrietta-Ann Le Clerc*, begun 1796. However, the present drawing is closest to the portrait reproduced by Sutherland Gower under the title '*Lady Antrobus*'. There is no mention of this sitter anywhere in Ward and Roberts; but in 1780 William Hayley, who was busy writing the *Triumphs of Temper* and had finished the first 3 books by September, was lent a house in Spring Gardens for a month in the late autumn. The lender was Mr Edmund Antrobus (see Chamberlain 99). There Hayley finished the poem. He may have prevailed upon his painter friend to recompense the lender.

58   Mother and child

Pen with grey ink and grey watercolour wash over pencil
213×257 mm ($8\frac{3}{8} \times 10\frac{1}{8}$ ins.)
Verso: inscribed in ink 'No. 56'

PROVENANCE: B.V. 59

REPRODUCED: Sutherland Gower, end plate, as 'Madonna'

The title is John Romney's. Possibly an early instance of the use of a favourite child model. From about 1782–86 Romney used the child of a guardsman as model (J.R. 146). He appeared in *Tragedy and Comedy nursing Shakespeare*, *The Infant Shakespeare attended by the Passions* and *Alope*, as well as in several projected, but unfinished works (e.g. *A group of Children in a Boat drifted out to sea*). John Romney states that the child died, thus frustrating the completion of several pictures. However Romney was so long in finishing fancy subjects that the child may simply have outgrown his part. Here the child appears to be about eight months old.

More important to him than the guardsman's son during this period 1782–6 was Emma Hart, his favourite and most famous model. Like most notorious characters, Emma probably helped to throw a veil over hear early career and make it as difficult as possible to chronicle. On 20 December 1791 Emma was to write to Romney, 'You was the first dear friend I open'd my heart to, you ought to know me, for you have seen and discoursed with me in my poorer days, you have known me in my poverty and prosperity' (quoted by Hugh Tours, *The Life and Letters of Emma Hamilton* [London, Gollancz, 1963] p. 96). It is tempting to wonder whether Romney had met Emma, perhaps in the capacity of a model, before 1782 when she came to live with the Honble. Charles Greville in a small house in Edgware Row, Paddington Green. Their orthography and their grammar were both bizarre. They spoke with similar North country accents, Romney from north and Emma from south Lancashire. They appear to have had great sympathy for each other. Greville had rescued the girl when she was thrown out of Uppark by her previous lover, Sir Harry Fetherstonhaugh. She was six months pregnant, and not yet seventeen. After the birth of the baby (which was immediately farmed out to its great-grandmother, old Mrs Kidd at Hawarden in Flintshire) Greville took Emma firmly in hand. He made her behave with decorum, and he began to educate her. He would not allow her to go about in public, but he did sanction frequent visits, no doubt chaperoned, to the painter's studio for portrait sittings. She appears very frequently in the sitters diaries from 1782–6 (although, unfortunately, that for 1785 is missing). It will be remembered that at this period Romney's friendship with the actor, John Henderson, was particularly close: they probably discussed Henderson's theories and practice of theatrical realism – the school of Sheridan rather than that of Garrick. This in its turn probably helped to shape Emma's notions of theatrical practice. It is evident that she soon discovered a talent for drama. Posing in Romney's studio, and talking about the subjects she was helping to depict, started her on the course which was to lead to the evolution of her famous 'Attitudes'. As a talented seventeen-year-old she was a stimulant to Romney's art. He was forty-eight and at the height of his powers: with Emma as an able and available model he revived many subjects previously attempted, but laid aside. For four years Emma was the centre of his subject paintings, and to devote more time to her he even appears to have cut down on the number of portrait sittings he accepted. It was sad for Romney that Greville, to suit his own purposes, got rid of Emma in 1786, packing her off to his uncle, Sir William Hamilton, in Naples. Emma thought she was merely going to have her voice trained, but what started as a summer expedition turned out to be a new life. She did not return for over five years, and then it was to marry Sir William. Romney lost his most successful model.

One can tell much about the relationship of painter and model from a draft letter which Romney wrote to her from Eartham in the summer of 1786 after she had first arrived in Naples. It is full of personal gossip – about his health, his paintings, his visit to Hayley – and it gives an impression of a very open and mutual friendship. Evidently Emma must have been an exceptionally intelligent and mature girl in matters of visualizing a dramatic scene: Romney asked her opinion of a new subject just suggested by Hayley: 'What do you think of it? I will expect to hear how you concive it.' The very thought of a new subject must have made him regret the loss of his best ally, for there immediately follows in the letter the most touching paragraph 'I have planned many other subjects for Pictures and flatter myself your goodness will indulge me with sitting when you return to England – I have had a great number of Ladys of figure sitting to me since you left England but all fall far short of the Spinstress indeed it is the Sun of my Hemisphear and they are but twinkling Stars – when I return to London I intend to finish the Cassandra and the Picture of Sensibility – the Baccanalian Picture is in statu quo allso the Serena and the Cibele and the Medea the last is the figure Setting with hair floating in the air— (Folger Shakespeare Library, leather bound sketch-book inscribed 'Letter', fol. 2 and fol. 2 *verso*).

59   Alope the Daughter of Cercyon

Pen with brown ink and grey watercolour wash over pencil (mostly erased)
360×516 mm ($14\frac{3}{16} \times 20\frac{5}{16}$ ins.)
Verso: inscribed in ink 'No. 176'

PROVENANCE: B.V. 86

REPRODUCED: Sutherland Gower, end plate as 'Sketch for painting of Lady Hamilton as Alope'

The title is that of John Romney: the painting for which this is a preparatory drawing is described in W. & R. II, 130 thus: 'Full-length figure half life-size; in red drapery, with left arm and shoulder bare, lying under some trees near a waterfall, and clasping a little child standing by her head; a lion and another wild beast in the distance.' Under the heading of paintings for which Emma modelled, John Romney lists '*Alope*; exposed with her child; bought by Admiral Vernon for sixty guineas' (J.R. 181). 'The lions were by Gilpin, and the picture was purchased by Admiral Vernon' (Robinson, quoted by J.R. 242–3). In the sketch-book which was formerly Truro No. 1, there are two receipts from Gilpin: '5 November 1783 £10:10:0' and '12 November 1783 £20'. There is a pencil sketch for *Alope* on the *verso* of a drawing for *The Initiation of a Rustic Nymph into the Rites of Bacchus* (B.V. 68 – see cat. no. 66). Probably the two subjects were being worked on at the same time. See also B.V. 100 *verso* and B.V. 143 *verso*.

60   Emma Hart as Medea slaying a child

Pen with brown ink and brown watercolour wash over pencil
400×310 mm ($15\frac{3}{4} \times 12\frac{3}{16}$ ins.)
Verso: inscribed at centre 'After 50'; inscribed lower right 'Fury' or 'Emy'

PROVENANCE: L.D. 149

EXHIBITED: *British Neo-Classical Art*, The National Trust, Ickworth, May–June 1969, No. 34; *Lady Hamilton* 1972, No. 7

This is a typical example of Romney's reworking a former pose, this time using Emma as model. It is only by comparison with the earlier version (see Smith College 1962, No. 44, repr. pl. XXVI) that the subject can really be identified. Here the body of the baby slung over the murderous Medea's back as she rides off in her chariot, is not clearly delineated. The sweetness of Emma's nature made her an inappropriate model in this instance. It is interesting to compare this drawing with cat. no. 10 to see how animated Romney's interpretation of Medea has now become: the drama is now theatrical rather than psychological. 'Mr Romney, Cavendish Square' appears in the subscriber's list of Dr Potter's two volume translation of the plays of Euripides which was published in 1781. The publication probably revived Romney's interest in the Medea story.

61   The Infancy of Shakespeare

Pen with brown ink and brown wash over pencil
307×497 mm ($12\frac{1}{8} \times 19\frac{9}{16}$ ins.)
Verso: pencil, partly worked over with pen and brown ink; a sketch for the same, but reversed (i.e. in the same sense as the Liverpool cartoon called by John Romney 'Infant Shakespeare'). Inscribed in ink 'No. 62'

PROVENANCE: B.V. 40

REPRODUCED: Sutherland Gower, end plate as 'First idea of the Infant Shakespeare nursed by Comedy and Tragedy'.

The composition is the reverse of the Liverpool cartoon. Yet John Romney dates *The Infant Shakespeare nursed by Tragedy and Comedy* 1791 (J.R. 219). The cartoon cannot be of that date. The surviving cartoons seem to belong to the period 1777–80. With the exception of *Odin before the Prophetess* and the two so-called Shakespeare ones, all illustrate classical subjects. The cartoon itself offers a puzzle: it is made up of sheets of handmade paper, pasted together, and the lowest sheet in the central section is in a different style from the rest. As several lines which traverse the join between it and the next sheet to the left do not flow continuously, and as the chalk background shading over the joins is overworked, it is possible that Romney redrew the lower central section and patched it with the cartoon later. The present drawing may connect with the revision of the cartoon. A strange vertical line brushed in to the upper left of the group, meaningless in the composition itself, appears to correspond with a join in the sheets of the Liverpool cartoon. Here may be an example of the reworking of a previous subject during the happy period when Emma Hart could model for him. The original subject of the cartoon may have been classical. In the sketch-book kept in

Florence in late January 1775 Romney noted as a subject suitable for a picture, 'a young Jupiter with his two women attendants'. He may have worked on this subject during or soon after his Italian visit. Like so many of his compositions it may have remained unfinished, or the subject may have lain fallow for a few years. All that we can be certain of is that in 1783, after the advent of Emma, he began to jot down ideas for *Young Jupiter*, showing the nanny goat from which he was fed as well as attendant women (sketch-book ex-collns. J. P. Haseltine, and Lord Nathan of Churt, sold Sotheby 14 November 1962, lot 50). He dated this book 'Septr 83' and the relevant sheets are fols. 4 *verso*, 5, 6, 7, 22, 23, 24, 35, 46, 47, 52, 56, 57, 57 *verso*, 58, 58 *verso*.

Later the same year he worked explicitly on the *Infancy of Shakespeare*. The cradle in which the child sits is inscribed in Romney's hand 'Shakes' (fol. 11). The relevant sketch-book was in the De Pass Collection and used to be known as Truro No. 1. The sketches, all in reverse of the present one, are on pages 9, 11, 13, 15, 17, 21. There are other related composition sketches in the Folger Shakespeare Library, L.B.V. 16 and L.B.V. 22. Page 10 of their rebound, interleaved sketch-book also bears a sketch for the composition, in pencil. See also Fitzwilliam Museum M.D. 47a and cat. no. 62a and 62b below.

The child in the composition is supposed to be the same as that in *Alope*, the guardsman's son (J.R. 146). Comedy is quite convincingly identified as Emma Hart.

62a   The Infant Shakespeare nursed by Comedy and Tragedy

Pencil
104 × 128 mm ($4\frac{1}{16} \times 5\frac{1}{16}$ ins.)

PROVENANCE: M.D. 26a

This appears to be an early composition trial for the subject. See notes on cat. no. 61 above. The inspiration may have come from a religious work such as Guido Reni's *Birth of the Virgin* (Quirinale, Rome, Chapel of the Annunciation); we know that Romney saw that work, for there is a drawing adapted from it in the Folger Shakespeare Library.

62b   Birth of Shakespeare

Pencil
193 × 199 mm ($7\frac{5}{8} \times 7\frac{7}{8}$ ins.)
Verso: pencil, woman sitting back on her haunches: inscribed in pencil '22' and 'Birth of Shakespere' (*sic*) and '71'

PROVENANCE: M.D. 26b *recto*

Compare Fitzwilliam Museum M.D. 47a, where a standing woman stretches her arms as though protectively above a small baby held on the lap of another woman. This was a motif used about 1791 for weird and sometimes rather sinister compositions in the Folger sketch-book inscribed 'Queen Mab'. Stylistically it seems preferable to date the present drawing around 1783: the recurrence of elements of the composition in studies of Queen Mab, the fairies' mid-wife is only another example of Romney's reviving an old idea in a new form.

63 Sketches for 'Lady Hamilton as Nature'

Brown watercolour wash over pencil
311×508 mm ($12\frac{1}{4} \times 20$ ins.)

PROVENANCE: L.D. 14

EXHIBITED: *Lady Hamilton* 1972, no. 4

The first work for which Emma sat to Romney was a three-quarter length portrait commissioned by Charles Greville. 'It was that beautiful one, so full of *naïvete*, in which she is represented with a little spaniel lap-dog under her arm.' (J.R. 180.) The first appointment listed for Emma is Friday 12 April at 11 o'clock. Between that date and 3 August there are thirteen more sittings in the diary for 1782. To this period the present sketches must belong. Movement was obviously the essence of Emma's nature, and so Romney catches her impetuously hurrying forward. In the finished painting (now in the Frick collection, New York) she carries the little dog under her left arm.

64 Group of Bacchantes assisting at the Initiation of a rustic nymph: two sketches

Sketch at left: pencil; sketch at right: pen with black ink and grey watercolour wash over traces of pencil (erased)
389×567 mm ($15\frac{5}{16} \times 22\frac{5}{16}$ ins.)
Verso: pencil: *Lady Hamilton as St Cecilia* (see George Paston, *George Romney* [London, Methuen, 1903], facing p. 102); and two others for a seated girl

PROVENANCE: B.V. 66

EXHIBITED: *Lady Hamilton* 1972, no. 9

There are, perhaps, more sketches for this subject than for any other at the same period. Credit for suggesting it is given to Richard Cumberland, whom

John Romney quotes: 'A group of Bacchantes are assisting at the initiation of a Rustic Nymph. They assail her senses with wine, music and dance; she hesitates; and in the moment betwixt the allurements of pleasure, and the simples of bashfulness, accepts the Thrysis in one hand, and seizes the goblet with the other. Triumph and revelry possess the whole group with every attitude of gaiety, every luxuriance of scenery enriches, and enflames the composition' (J.R. 260). At various stages of the composition the morphology of Emma appears in both the nymph and the priestess. Moreover in Truro sketch-book no. 2, dated 'June 84 from January' there were four sketches for the group of bacchante and nymph, the one urging the other forwards (pages 64, 78, 79 and 80) as well as a series for the portrait of Emma as a Bacchante (pages 50, 51, 66, 70, 71, 80, 83). Evidently Romney worked on both subjects simultaneously. Emma was his greatest preoccupation at the time. The Bacchanalian subjects sadly presage her latter days when an addiction to alcohol was added to her other notorieties.

The painting of the Initiation was never finished. A facetious remark of Captain Thomas Dalton discouraged him – or so John Romney would have us believe (the son goes to much trouble to suggest external factors which could have hindered the completion of many of his father's favourite designs). 'When Captain Thomas Dalton, a gentleman remarkable for turning everything to burlesque, was sitting to him for his portrait, he unfortunately cast his eye upon a large picture that Mr Romney was engaged with and which was considerably advanced. The subject was the Initiation of a Virgin into the mysteries of Bacchus, in which ceremony a number of graceful females were engaged. I have forgot what the precise observation was which he made; but it gave such a ludicrous, and unchaste turn to the design, that Mr Romney too readily yielded to the impression, and the picture was forever laid aside.' (J.R. 57.) It is impossible to tell when the Captain made his damaging remark. Two 'Capt. Dalton's' occur in the diaries, one the father (John) and the other the facetious son. The first session in April, May, June and July 1782 probably refers to the father; the second, February 1783, to the son. The diary for 1785 is lost: had Dalton sat that year the dates could have fitted better. Romney certainly continued to work on the subject in 1784. Of course the story may be apocryphal, another instance of John Romney's extenuating a perennial failing of his father, the inability to finish works.

65   Rustic Nymph for 'Initiation of a Rustic Nymph'

Pen with brown ink and grey watercolour wash over pencil
513 × 306–327 mm (20$\frac{3}{16}$ × 12$\frac{1}{8}$–12$\frac{3}{8}$ ins.)
Verso: pencil; group either for *Initiation of a Rustic Nymph* or for *Fortune Telling*; inscribed in ink 'No. 37'

PROVENANCE: B.V. 74

EXHIBITED: *Lady Hamilton* 1972, no. 11

See cat. no. 64. The two figures most closely resemble Truro sketch-book no. 2, pages 78 and 79.

66   Priestess for 'Initiation of a Rustic Nymph'

Pen with brown ink and grey watercolour wash over pencil
386×563 mm ($15\frac{1}{4} \times 22\frac{3}{16}$ ins.)
Verso: pencil sketch for *Alope* (see cat. no. 59 above) inscribed in ink
'No. 96'

PROVENANCE: B.V. 68

EXHIBITED: *Lady Hamilton* 1972, no. 10

See notes on cat. no. 64

67   Sketches for Priestess and Novitiate

Pen with brown ink
292×445 mm ($11\frac{1}{2} \times 17\frac{1}{2}$ ins.)

PROVENANCE: L.D. 144

The style of these preliminary pen sketches is very difficult to date. Compare this sheet both with cat. no. 24, which can be firmly dated 1776, and with Truro no. 1 which can be firmly dated to 1782. We can only say of the present sheet that it shows Romney's interest in the confrontation of Priestess and female novitiate. In one sketch the Priestess pours a libation and the novitiate appears overcome with grief rather than bacchic frenzy.

68   Sketches for classical figures, possibly mourning

Pen with pale brown ink
289×445 mm ($11\frac{3}{8} \times 17\frac{1}{2}$ ins.)

PROVENANCE: L.D. 143

The sheet is entirely comparable with L.D. 144 (cat. no. 67 above). Date and subject are uncertain while, stylistically, it spans the period from 1776 to the

advent of Emma Hart who animated many subjects which Romney had long
been considering.

69 Composition drawing for 'The Spinstress'

Pen with brown ink and grey watercolour wash over pencil
392 × 294 mm ($15\frac{7}{16}$ × $11\frac{9}{16}$ ins.)
Verso: inscribed in ink 'No. 54'

PROVENANCE: B.V. 85

REPRODUCED: Sutherland Gower, end plate as 'First idea of the Painting
of Lady Hamilton Spinning'; *Country Life*, vol. CXXIX, no. 3355,
22.vi.1961, p. 1477, fig. 5

EXHIBITED: Kenwood, 1961, no. 44; *Lady Hamilton* 1972, no. 13

LITERATURE: W. & R. II, 186 under *Lady Hamilton at the Spinning
Wheel*, notes the existence of this drawing

Design for the full-length life-sized painting in oils (canvas 68 × 50, the
Iveagh Bequest, Kenwood) for Emma as '*The Spinstress*'. The painting was
placed as No. 8 in John Romney's list of portraits of Emma painted by his
father (J.R. 181). It was 'bought by Mr Curwen for one hundred and fifty
guineas'. John Romney quotes an opinion of Robinson, who studied under
Romney about 1785, 'Perhaps the Girl spinning is the best picture he painted
at this period; he first caught the idea from observing a cobbler's wife sitting
in a stall' (J.R. 243). The painting was originally intended for Charles
Greville, but was not finished until after Emma Hart had gone to Naples.
Greville then relinquished his claim on the painting – for his declared ease
of both mind and pocket – to Mr Christian Curwen (J.R. 184–6 where
Greville's letter is quoted). The picture had been entirely finished when
Greville renounced his claim, 25 February 1788.

70 Spinning woman with two small children

Pen with brown ink and grey watercolour wash over pencil
386 × 340 mm ($15\frac{3}{16}$ × $13\frac{3}{8}$ ins.)

PROVENANCE: B.V. 116

LITERATURE: Chamberlain 364

John Romney identifies this composition as 'A Mother and two daughters; a
sketch for portraits' (J.R. 264). If an actual group portrait was ever painted
on this model, it is lost – sadly, for the composition has great potential charm
and originality.

71 A shepherd boy asleep, watched by his dog at the approach of a thunderstorm

Grey watercolour wash over black chalk
270×300 mm (10$\frac{5}{8}$×11$\frac{13}{16}$ ins.)
Verso: black chalk, partly erased, lower half probably of full-face portrait drawing of lady with right hand stretched down by her side

PROVENANCE: L.D. 145

John Romney mentions this composition when listing fancy pictures unfinished for want of models: 'He had a servant boy with a fine countenance, whom he had begun to employ as a model for a picture representing *A Shepherd Boy asleep watched by his Dog at the approach of a thunder-storm.* This was one of those natural subjects, in which Gainsborough so much excelled and from the promise that this picture gave in so early a stage, I am confident that had it been finished, it would have ranked with the best works of that master, or with those of Murillo; but unluckily, the lad having been guilty of some misconduct, was hastily dismissed, and the picture was never afterwards touched' (J.R. 146).

There is another version of the composition in the Fitzwilliam collection (L.D. 146).

72 Portrait sketch for a standing woman in a landscape with a waterfall

Grey watercolour wash over black chalk
498×295–298 mm (19$\frac{5}{8}$×11$\frac{5}{8}$–11$\frac{3}{4}$ ins.)

PROVENANCE: L.D. 65

The composition is distinctive and unusual with its strong diagonal cross axis and the waterfall in the close background. I am only sorry to be one of those who does not know the finished painting. The hair style and dress are those of 1779–81 – see for instance *the Honble Mrs Trevor* 1779–80, and *the Countess of Westmorland* 1780–2.

In many ways the years when Emma Hart modelled regularly for him were the happiest and most settled in Romney's career. He was an established portraitist, 'Reynolds and Romney divide the town,' declared Lord Thurlow, Lord High Chancellor of England, 'I am of the Romney faction' (J.R. 172). That was the sweet sound of success. It was late in 1780 that Thurlow had come into Romney's life, introduced by Lord Gower who wished his friend's portrait painted. Thurlow, an amateur of classical literature, obviously delighted in discussing subjects with Romney and introduced the story of Orpheus and Eurydice from Virgil's fourth *Georgic*. The Lord Chancellor obligingly supplied

Romney with his own translation of the tragic return from the Underworld, and added notes on how he visualized the scene (J.R. 168–172). He appears to have kept an active interest in Romney long after the portrait sittings were over for on 26 April 1789, John Romney was to be instituted Rector of Southery, Norfolk, which was in the gift of the Lord Chancellor.

The success of John's academic career added to Romney's pleasure. It must have been gratifying to have his only son respectably settled in Cambridge, and secretly Romney could rejoice that the tiresome and unsympathetic young man was firmly established a good way from London. (See *Admissions to the College of St John the Evangelist in the University of Cambridge*, Part IV, July 1767–July 1802. Edited by Sir Robert Forsyth Scott [Cambridge, Printed for the College at the University Press, 1931], p. 455.)

His other contemporary biographer, William Hayley, was by this time also a regular part of Romney's life. In 1780 Hayley wrote his one great success, *The Triumphs of Temper*, a didactic poem instructing young ladies in allegorical fashion, how to retain a sweet nature and good temper against all odds. Emma Hart declared that she owed Hayley thanks for the lessons she had learnt from reading the poem. After her marriage she wrote to Romney from Caserta on 20 December 1791 and said 'Give my love to Mr Hayley, tell him I shall be glad to see him at Naples . . . I am always reading his *Triumphs of Temper*; it was that that made me Lady H., for, God knows, I had for five years enough to try my temper and I am affraid if it had not been for the good example Serena taught me, my girdle would have burst, and if it had I had been undone for Sir W. minds more temper than beauty. He, therefore, wishes Mr Hayley would come, that he might thank him for his sweet-tempered wife. I swear to you I have never been once out of humour since the 6th of last September' (Alfred Morrison, *The Collection of Autograph Letters and Historical Documents formed by Alfred Morrison* (second series 1882–92); *The Hamilton & Nelson Papers*, 2 vols, London, privately printed, 1893 & 1894, I, pp. 158–9). Several of the many editions of the poem are illustrated with plates said on the engravings to be after designs by Stothard: however at least three are definitely from designs by Romney, probably made in 1780–3. One cannot help recalling the bitter disagreement between Blake and Stothard about the engraving of the *Canterbury Pilgrims* (see A. C. Coxhead, *Thomas Stothard, R.A., an Illustrated monograph* [London, A. H. Bullen, 1906] pp. 21–4).

Four years later Hayley began work on his extraordinary *Essay on Old Maids*, a three volume prose work first published in December 1785. Romney, on his regular summer visits to Eastham, may have started work on illustrations as early as 1784. Several exist even in the John Romney Gift; yet the illustrated third edition which appeared in 1793 has, like the *Triumphs of Temper*, plates after designs attributed in the engraved credits entirely to Stothard. The *Essay on Old Maids*, because of its very matter, is said to have done Hayley's reputation much harm (see Bishop, pp. 89–90). Perhaps Romney, though he made the designs, did not want to be associated with book illustration: John Romney was always acid about this book in particular. In the manuscript catalogue of his Gift he refers to 'Mr Hayley's Essay on Old Maids, a work unworthy of the honour thus done it (by his father's illustrations) & which ought rather to have been consigned to oblivion'. Thirteen years later, when he published Romney's biography he had changed the entry to 'These eight sheets are taken from Mr Hayley's Essay on

Old-Maids. A work which reflects no credit on its author, whatever merit it may have had in suggesting these designs.' (J.R. 262.) It is not surprising that Hayley lost friends when he published the work: it bristles with comments on, for instance, the 'many virgins . . . who, with the heavy wing of the beetle, affect the sportive motions of the butterfly'. (*Essay on Old Maids*, vol. I, p. 55) Though it claims to be a eulogy on spinsterhood, its general effect is the reverse.

73 Kunaza delivers the child to his mother, Kezia

Pen with grey ink and grey watercolour wash over pencil (mostly erased)
372×493 mm ($14\frac{5}{8} \times 19\frac{7}{16}$ ins.)
Verso: inscribed in ink 'No. 111'

PROVENANCE: B.V. 95

The subject is taken from William Hayley's *Essay on old Maids*, vol. II, pp. 14–37 and occurs in what purports to be a translation of a fragment from the writings of Enoch. It tells of Pharmarus one of the corrupt angels who, though set to watch over the earth, had forgotten their duty and 'begot a multitude of giants upon the daughters of men'. He attempts to corrupt Kunaza, the virgin daughter of Enoch, using as one of his arguments, the beauty of the child born to Kezia, the seventieth daughter of Enoch, and Semiexas, the leader of this band of rebel angels: 'and this was the first Anack that was born upon the earth. And Kunaza beheld the infant, and was astonished in surveying its stature. She embraced the babe with amazement, and she delighted in the magnitude of its limbs! And she delivered the babe to its mother Kezia, and she observed the proud transport of the mother in contemplating the dimensions of the child. . . .' (p. 23). However, Kunaza does not succumb to Pharmarus (shown at the right, looking upon the scene with intense hope). If anything were wanted to prove that Romney was not inspired by literature itself, but rather by the enthusiasm of his various friends for literary subjects, the fact that he illustrated the *Essay on Old Maids* could be put forward as powerful evidence. One can sympathise on this occasion with John Romney who describes the story of the daughters of Enoch as 'an Antediluvean fragment . . . which offends by the affectation of scriptural language'. (J.R. 262)

The composition may be compared with that of *The Infancy of Shakespeare* (see cat. no. 61) on which he had worked shortly before.

There are three versions of the subject in the John Romney Gift, nos. B.V. 93, B.V. 94, and the present drawing. In order of composition, this one appears to be the earliest.

Sketches for subjects from an *Essay on Old Maids* occur in sketch-book 'B' of a private collection in Pennsylvania; the same sketch-book also contains drawings for the *Initiation of a Rustic Nymph*.

The medium used here is that generally associated with preparing a composition for engraving. It appears to have been the model for the frontispiece to vol. II of the third edition, published in 1793. The design of the published plate is credited on the engravings to Stothard.

74 The Rape of Kunaza

Pen with grey ink and grey watercolour wash over pencil (mostly erased)
386 × 576 mm (15$\frac{3}{16}$ × 22$\frac{11}{16}$ ins.)
Verso: inscribed in ink 'No. 66'

PROVENANCE: B.V. 97

See previous notes and cat. no. 73. The subject, from Hayley's *Essay on Old Maids*, Vol. II, p. 35 is Pharmarus' final attempt on Kunaza, the virgin daughter of Enoch. 'And he grasped the virgin with the vehement grasp of outrageous desire: and she shrieked aloud in the agonies of terror. And at the sound of her shriek, the angel Gabriel alighted upon the earth: Pharmarus saw him, and was abashed for a moment.' He is overcome by Gabriel.

Despite his intense dislike of the book, John Romney rather surprisingly says of the present composition 'The Rape of Kunaza ... is designed with all the force and spirit of Raffaelle.' (J.R. 262) However, it was not used to illustrate the third edition as was cat. no. 73. Even so, the medium used here is that associated with preparation of a design for print making.

At the end of the second week of March 1786, having packed two last sittings to Romney into the first half of the month (March 1 and 8), Emma set out for Naples accompanied by her mother. For a travelling companion on the first half of the journey – that is, to Geneva – they had the painter Gavin Hamilton. Romney was left with a studio full of portrait sketches of Emma, and unfinished paintings. He wrote cheerfully to her of his intentions of finishing some of these. Hayley was a great comfort. He spent a month in London, from October to November, at the painter's house. On 2 November he rode out to Mr Lea the famous nursery man at Hammersmith, in order to buy a 'sensitive plant' of the size to suit the picture Romney was finishing, Emma as *Sensibility* (Hayley papers, Fitzwilliam Museum, XIX, William Hayley to Eliza, 2 Nov. 1786).

But soon a far greater plan was underway, and one which was to preoccupy Romney for at least the next six years.

It is difficult to unravel the claims and counterclaims for the origin of the Boydell Shakespeare Gallery. The idea chimed with the times. It was so obviously what England and the age needed, that many of those involved honestly believed the initial idea to be their own. George Nicol declared in the 1802 *Advertisement* for the Boydell Shakespeare Gallery that he had thought of the idea. John Romney maintains that George Romney was the prime mover: 'the idea of it originated from himself individually: he had often ruminated on it in his solitary hours; for he had always regarded Shakespeare as an author abounding in those picturesque conceptions and representations which may be so easily transferred to the canvas by an imaginative painter' (J.R. 151). Certainly the scheme was under way by 13 December 1786, when William Hayley wrote to Thomas Green from Eartham:

'My dear Greene,

   Accept my cordial thanks for the Shakespeare papers & for yr. pleasing Account of the success which so justly attends that noble project – I trust you and Long will spur our dear Romney's Ambition to keep pace with the National Enthusiasm – remind him frequently that *He was the Prime Mover* of this grand undertaking; & that He should paint accordingly.' (Letter among the Dawson Green papers.)

   There had been a dinner, apparently at Josiah Boydell's. Present at the dinner were Josiah's uncle, Alderman Boydell the print seller, George Nicol the publisher and printer, Benjamin West, George Romney, Paul Sandby, Daniel Braithwaite, Romney's old friend and patron from the Post Office, Hoole the translator of Ariosto, and the ubiquitous William Hayley. John Romney was mistaken in placing the dinner as late as 1787: it must have taken place in November or early December 1786, as we see from Hayley's letter to Thomas Greene (quoted above). Romney made a quick start on his *Tempest* painting: John Romney even suggests that he may have begun work on the composition before the dinner, and that it may have been this which turned the conversation to Shakespeare (J.R. 151). Romney then broached his 'plan of a National Gallery of pictures painted from that great dramatist, which would be both honourable to the country, and to the poet, and contribute essentially to the advancement of historical painting' (J.R. *ibid.*). John Boydell, a good businessman, elaborated on the plan and proposed to 'establish an *English School of Historial Painting*' by commissioning from all the best living British artists paintings on subjects drawn exclusively from the plays of Shakespeare. From these paintings prints were to be made, the paintings themselves remaining on public exhibition in the Shakespeare Gallery. Concurrently an edition of Shakespeare was to be produced by 'Mr Nicol, his Majesty's Bookseller, whose zeal for the improvement of Printing in this country is well known.' (John Boydell in the *Preface*, dated 1 May 1789, to the first *Catalogue of the Pictures &c. in the Shakespeare Gallery, Pall-Mall.*) Everything was launched under the best auspices. Even Sir Joshua Reynolds agreed to contribute although, good businessman as he was, he insisted on a higher fee (one thousand guineas) than anyone else received: Romney, neither a good businessman nor a politician, may have felt slighted when he was only given six hundred guineas for *The Tempest*. John Romney was aggrieved (J.R. 152).

   Boydell was astute. The venture seemed bound to be a glittering success. English prints had a wide market, even on the Continent, thanks largely to Boydell himself. 'When I began the business of publishing and selling Prints, all the fine Engravings sold in England were imported from foreign countries, particularly from France. – Happily, the reverse is now the case; for few are imported, and many are exported, to a great annual amount' (John Boydell, *op. cit.* iii and iv). The fatal flaw in the situation, still unseen in May 1789, was the French Revolution. Boydell was to die on the verge of bankruptcy.

   Keener, perhaps, than any other present at that original planning dinner,

47

Romney entered on the Boydell Shakespeare venture with high hopes. But the strain on him, at the age of 52, was enormous. He already had heavy commitments to portraiture; and now he attempted simultaneously to work as a history or subject painter like West. In February 1787 he wrote to Hayley, 'I have now entered upon a new plan, and must fight through it with all my might. Do not think I despair! but I find it necessary to gather all the assistance I can collect from my friends, as I have so very little time, either to think or read for myself. This cursed portrait-painting! How I am shackled with it! I am determined to live frugally, that I may enable myself to cut it short, as soon as I am tolerably independent, and then give my mind up to those delightful regions of imagination' (W.H. 123). The effort may have been too much for him. It took four years to complete his first painting, *The Tempest*, and it was not a success. Joseph Farington noted in his diary for 17 July 1794: 'Boyer is afraid of employing Romney, on account of the unpopularity of his Tempest Picture in the Shakespeare Gallery.'

It was these very years in which Romney's political beliefs were also sadly shaken. Commerce and idealism together let him down. Disillusioned on both scores, he was assailed by a nervous desire to retreat from the world. His works for the Shakespeare Gallery were the last history pictures in which his professional aspirations were publicly engaged.

75   Prospero, Miranda and Caliban

Grey watercolour wash over pencil
388 × 454 mm ($15\frac{5}{16}$ × $17\frac{7}{8}$ ins.)
Verso: pencil; Prospero and Miranda at right, scribbled indication of the storm and shipwreck at left

PROVENANCE: L.D. 95

The composition was Romney's first idea for depicting the storm scene in the *Tempest*: Prospero, Miranda and Caliban together on the island, watching the rising storm. Sometimes he experimented with reversing figures or re-adjusting them slightly, but on the whole the design was satisfactory and manageable. However, it did not satisfy Romney or his friends' grandiose ideas. John Romney, who bitterly resented the excessive hours his father spent on *The Tempest*, reported impatiently that, 'some officious individual suggested to Mr Romney that this picture would not be regarded by the critics as an historical composition, as it consisted of only three figures not sufficiently combined' (J.R. 153). There is another of these early three figure versions in the Fitzwilliam (B.V. 120), but in it the group is reversed.

In designing the figure of Miranda, Romney drew upon his stock of sketches of Emma Hart. The head in the final version, close to the attitude shown on the reverse of this sheet, is drawn from a beautiful oil sketch now in the Philadelphia Museum of Art (see *Lady Hamilton*, 1972, no. 18).

76 The Tempest: Alonso King of Naples and Mariners

Pen with black ink and grey watercolour wash over pencil
287 × 360 mm (11$\frac{5}{16}$ × 14$\frac{3}{16}$ ins.)

PROVENANCE: L.D. 108

This sketch is for the final version of the subject, although no figure exactly corresponds. Romney chose to depict not a dramatic incident from the stage, but a piece of reported drama, the moment when the king's son, Ferdinand, leaps overboard at the height of the storm. Romney shows his frantic father rushing forward in an agony to save him, and courtiers or mariners holding him back. In his rough draughts he was attempting to capture the utmost turbulence. The composition of this group was probably suggested by Raphael's *Sacrifice at Lystra*. It seems that Hayley was bear-leading Romney at this stage of the evolution of the painting. He pompously tells us how he nursed the painter along: 'Romney justly imagined that it would aid and inspirit him in his great undertaking, to make a fresh survey of Raphael's cartoons . . .' and for that purpose they made a special trip to Windsor in the autumn of 1787 (W.H. 132).

It was a mammoth undertaking, particularly for a professional portrait painter. The final canvas, measuring 9 foot 10$\frac{1}{2}$ inches by 15 foot 3 inches, contained eighteen figures, almost all in a state of extreme activity, and many partially naked.

The final painting has now perished, and only a few heads cut from it survive in the Civic Museum and Art Gallery, Bolton, Lancashire.

77a Head of Alonso for 'The Tempest'

Pencil
142 × 111 mm (5$\frac{9}{16}$ × 4$\frac{3}{8}$ ins.)

PROVENANCE: M.D. 19a

The wild-eyed King, lunging forward to clutch his son as he jumps overboard appears to be derived from a study of the head of Hayley. John Romney reports 'Mr Hayley had sat as the model for Prospero' (J.R. 151) and Hayley himself admits to generally 'assisting him in the humble capacity of a painters layman' throughout his work on *The Tempest* during the last months of 1788 (W.H. 136). His face stamps its image, narrow cheek-bones and long nose, on many of *The Tempest* sketches.

77b Head study

Pencil
141 × 111 mm (5$\frac{9}{16}$ × 4$\frac{3}{8}$ ins.)

The head expresses horror, rather than malevolence. It is similar to M.D. 40a, but can also be compared to studies for the head of a Fiend (see cat. no. 81 and no. 82). Stylistically it, too, dates from the years when Romney worked for the Boydell Shakespeare Gallery.

78   Margery Jourdain and Bolingbroke conjuring up the Fiend

Pen with grey ink and grey watercolour wash over pencil
382–379 × 559–562 mm ($15\frac{1}{16}$–$14\frac{15}{16}$ × 22–$22\frac{1}{8}$ ins.)

PROVENANCE: B.V. 135

The title is John Romney's. The incident comes from *Henry VI* Part II, Act I, sc. iv. Margery Jourdain, Southwell and Bolingbroke meet in Gloucester's garden; Hume, the second priest accompanies the Duchess of Gloucester upon the battlements to watch the proceedings. *Bolingbroke:* 'Mother Jourdain, be you prostrate and grovel on the earth; John Southwell, read you; and let us to our work.' They raise the Fiend and question him about the fate of the King, the Duke of Suffolk and the Duke of Somerset. This drawing even indicates the battlements, with the Duchess of Gloucester and her companion above. It is a development of the subject later than B.V. 133. In B.V. 134 the composition and figures are the reverse of here, and no battlements or figures above are shown. There is a sketch for Bolingbroke on the *verso* of L.D. 133 (Miss Wallis as *Mirth and Melancholy*, a picture also painted in 1788). Many sketches for the subject were in a sketch-book once belonging to Lord Nathan of Churt. This had various inscriptions, including 'August 1788' and 'Witchcraft'. It was foliated from the opposite end: 127 *verso*, 127, 123 (Duchess of Gloucester), 122 *verso* (Bolingbroke), 121 *verso* (Bolingbroke), 114 *verso* (Fiend), 114 (Fiend), 113 *verso* (Fiend), 59, 58, 23 (Bolingbroke and Southwell), 22, 21 *verso*, 5 *verso*, 4. For the Fiend there are several fine head studies (see cat. nos. 80, 81 and 82 as well as Folger Shakespeare Library, Portfolio 24). Among other studies, the Folger also has a full composition drawing in watercolour wash (L.B.V. 48) and a pencil study of Bolingbroke (L.B.V. 17).

One great complaint that Romney and other artists could justly level against the Boydell Gallery was that there was no control over the allocation of subject matter. It is true that Romney had opted for the storm scene in *The Tempest*, and so no one took that on. It was equally true that Reynolds had been given an advance payment for *Macbeth and the Witches* – a subject Romney would also have liked for himself. But it seems that in the case of other subjects it was a free-for-all: Romney was frustrated in his hopes of painting *Margery Jourdain and Bolingbroke conjuring up the Fiend*, even although he had worked out a powerful composition which he might have handled admirably. John Opie beat him to it, finishing his painting of the same subject *Bolingbroke consults Mother Jourdain* first. Opie was twenty-seven years younger than Romney, a relative newcomer, and not one of England's established or best artists. Romney became disillusioned (J.R. 154).

79   Head of Bolingbroke

Pencil
287 × 262 mm ($11\frac{5}{16} × 10\frac{5}{16}$ ins.)
Verso: inscribed in pencil lower right 'Lapland witch'; pencil sketch for three figures at right pointing at fourth figure at extreme left. The composition is reminiscent of the meeting of Macbeth and the three witches as shown in the Henderson portrait.

PROVENANCE: L.D. 80

The head is a study for Bolingbroke in B.V. 135 (see cat. no. 78), and as such should be dated 1788–90 when Romney was doing his most concentrated work for the Boydell Shakespeare Gallery.

80   Hag or Fiend

Pencil
252 × 104 mm ($9\frac{15}{16} × 4\frac{1}{8}$ ins.)

PROVENANCE: M.D. 14

Although the general effect is more timorous and hag-like, the way the head is shrunk between the shoulders, and the hair flies up on end is exactly like the Fiend raised by Margery Jourdain (see cat. no. 78).

81   Study for the Fiend's Head (1)

Black chalk worked with stump over traces of pencil; strengthened with black chalk
303 × 300 mm ($11\frac{15}{16} × 11\frac{13}{16}$ ins.)

PROVENANCE: B.V. 136

John Romney's identification is convincing. See *Margery Jourdain and Bolingbroke conjuring up the Fiend*, B.V. 135 (cat. no. 78) for which this is a study.

82 Study for the Fiend's Head (2)

Black chalk and brown chalk worked with stump, strengthened with black chalk

$521 \times 370–376$ mm ($20\frac{1}{2} \times 14\frac{9}{16}–14\frac{13}{16}$ ins.)

Verso: black chalk, a sketch for the Fiend's head, and two details of the mouth

PROVENANCE: B.V. 137

When working on historical or literary subjects Romney gave clear evidence of his training as a portrait painter. His studies for heads are always most impressive, as here, where he elaborates on an already impressive study. Among the study material available to him as a very young man was a copy of Le Brun's *Passions*. Unfortunately difficulties often arose when he had to leave the heads and progress to full-length figures in dramatic action.

In April 1790 Romney finally succeeded in finishing *The Tempest* to his own satisfaction. The emotional stress of creating such an enormous work in a genre so unfamiliar to him, was enervating. Moreover the painting was bound for public exhibition, a trial he had not undergone since his return from France fifteen years before. It was soon evident to his friends that he needed a change of scene. One friend in particular was both enthusiastic about *The Tempest* and in a position to offer the artist an especially fascinating holiday. The Rev. John Warner had been living in rooms in Barnard's Inn for three years past, and there had had many friendly visits from Romney and Hayley. Now he had just been appointed domestic chaplain to young Lord Gower, elder brother of Lady Anne Leveson, the sixteen year old with the tambourine painted by Romney in the *Dancing Gower Children* (see cat. no. 19). And young Lord Gower was England's new ambassador in Paris. On 31 July 1790 Romney, Hayley and the Rev. Thomas Carwardine set out from Eartham to stay with John Warner.

The French Revolution was just one year old. Europe was in a ferment of speculation about events in Paris. Romney was a natural Radical. His friend, John Warner was 'somewhat imbued with revolutionary ideas' (Thompson Cooper on John Warner, *Dictionary of National Biography*). Yet the only published accounts of the holiday speak not of revolutionary France, but of festivities, dinner parties at Lord Gower's and outings to see paintings. It must be an instance of tactful editing after the event.

However Romney's prime concern remained with pictures: 'the first morning after his arrival in Paris, was employed in a visit to the Orleans collection' (W.H. 145). He was going over the same ground as he had on his visit with Thomas Greene twenty-six years before: it must have made him acutely aware of the passage of time. His ambition to succeed as a history painter was still far from fulfilled. He strengthened his resolution to make even greater efforts. Moreover he was impressed by the work of contemporary French artists. A visit to the Luxembourg must have reminded him of artists who were so close to the political events of their day that their works became allegories of contemporary history: 'the Splendour of Rubens did not strike us blind to the merit of David' said

Hayley (W.H. 149). At the same time Hayley particularly mentioned how impressed they were by David's *Death of Socrates*, *Paris and Helen* and the *Oath of the Horatii*. Both Greuze and David had occasion to dine with the party. Romney must have noticed how close to the heart of things contemporary art and artists in France were. Idealism ran high. 'It was a time when that scene of astonishing vicissitudes presented to the friends of peace, of freedom and of the arts, a spectacle of cheerful curiosity, and of hope so magnificent in promises of good to mankind, that philanthropy could not fail to exult in the recent prospect, unconscious that the splendid vision was destined to sink in the most execrable horrors of barbarity and blood' (W.H. 143).

Idealistic altruism and reforming zeal were represented in one particular topic on which they must all have talked during the visit – how to raise a fitting memorial to John Howard. In his monumental surveys, *The state of the Prisons in England and Wales* (Warrington, 1777) and *The Principal Lazarettos in Europe* (Warrington, 1789) Howard had drawn attention to the appalling conditions in which prisoners were incarcerated throughout Europe. Here were grounds for revolutionary protest laid bare. His books probably supplied visions of captivity and death to many people who had never seen the inside of a cell, let alone a corpse-littered room. Now Howard himself had died of gaol fever at Kherson, in South Russia in the early months of 1790. As long ago as 1786 Warner had instigated a scheme to erect a public statue to Howard for his pioneer work on prison reform: but Howard, who hated publicity, had blocked all such plans during his lifetime.

The crossing back to England on August 21st was very bad. From Dieppe to Brighton took twenty-two hours; Romney reported: 'it rained all the time and was very hot' (J.R. 218). He was very ill, and his sickness continued for two weeks after their return to Eartham. The new inspirations which came out of the Paris visit must all have taken a sombre colouring. Hayley's robust enthusiasm immediately carried him into work on his *Eulogies of Howard, a Vision* which he presented, gratuitously, to his publisher, Johnson, the following year. Romney began to draw new subjects taken from 'scenes of human wretchedness which might have been supposed to have met the eye of the philanthropist, Howard, in his perilous visits to the Lazarettos and prisons abroad' (J.R. 266).

83   Joan of Arc upon the walls of Rouen

Pen with brown ink and pale brown ink wash over pencil
495 × 308–311 mm (19½ × 12⅛–12¼ ins.)
Verso: pencil, seated woman full face with a small child (?holding a book) standing at left: inscribed in ink 'After 50' and 'Ceres'

PROVENANCE: L.D. 153

The subject is from Shakespeare's *Henry VI* part I, act III sc. ii: *Enter La Pucelle on the top, thrusting out a torch burning*

> 'Behold this is the happy wedding torch
>   That joineth Rouen unto her countrymen,
>   But burning fatal to the Talbotites!' (Exit)

After his return from France in 1790, Romney was ill spasmodically for most of the winter. Hayley tried to rally his spirits by suggesting suitable subjects for major historical paintings. On 3 May 1791 Romney was to write to him, 'I am obliged to you for the subjects you have pointed out . . . for the present I have fixt on Joan La Pucelle making her incantation, and another I intend from her appearance on the walls of Rouen, with a torch in her hand' (W.H. 157). In the National Gallery of Scotland, Edinburgh, there is a sheet (D. 4657) on the *recto* of which are two sketches, that at the right, in pencil alone, being the same figure we have here. At the left of the Edinburgh sheet taking up approximately half its width is a sketch drawn in dark brown wash over indications in pencil, showing a half-kneeling figure recoiling before a spirit which rises from the ground. This sheet I identify as *Joan of Arc making her incantation*, and *Joan of Arc upon the walls of Rouen*. The Fitzwilliam drawing is a more developed version of the equivalent figure on the Edinburgh sheet, and both should be dated 1791. John Romney says that the Joan of Arc composition, presumably the present one, was to be modelled on Emma. She returned to London in late May 1791 and stayed until, on 6 September, she married Sir William Hamilton. The Joan of Arc was to be a companion to the Cassandra (J.R. 154). On 19 June 1791, Romney, delighted at last because his favourite model had returned, wrote to Hayley 'I dedicate my time to this charming lady: . . . The pictures I have begun, are Joan of Arc, a Magdalene, and a Bacchante for the Prince of Wales; and another I am to begin as a companion to the Bacchante. I am also to paint a picture of Constance for the Shakespeare Gallery' (W.H. 159).

84   Banquet scene, Macbeth

Pencil

122 × 192 mm ($4\frac{13}{16} \times 7\frac{9}{16}$ ins.)

PROVENANCE: L.D. 68

As a trimmed leaf from a sketch-book, this is typical of Romney's initial work on a subject in the 1790s. Hayley dates Romney's work on the Banquet Scene in *Macbeth* to the spring of 1792, 'but suspecting that the proprietors of the Gallery were not inclined to encourage his intention, though he often employed himself in slight sketches of the subject, I believe he never made any farther advance in the picture'. (W.H. 172–3) There are sketches in earlier sketch-books, for instance the one from Lord Nathan of Churt's collection dated 'Spring 1791' (fols. 34 *verso*, 35, 36, 48, 49, 50, 100) which occur side by side with studies for Howard subjects. In the Folger Shakespeare Library there is another such sketch-book, inscribed 'Macbeth / Midsummernight dream / McBeth' (fols. 12, 13, 14, 15, 17, 18, 49, 50, 51, 52, 53, 57, 59, 61, 63, 64, 65). The Folger sketch-book contains, besides Howard and *Midsummer Night's Dream* subjects, sketches for Joan of Arc compositions.

There are other, and larger, *Banquet Scene* sketches in the Fitzwilliam and in the Folger. That Romney's imagination was extremely vivid, and worked in an almost cinematographic manner, can be seen from the consecutive draughts of this subject: as the Ghost of Banquo approaches, Macbeth reacts more and more vigorously, Lady Macbeth's efforts to restrain him become greater, and the guests reel back in confusion and surprise. Romney was drawing at great speed and the resulting compositions are dynamic and well knit.

85 The Ghost of Banquo

Pencil
369·5 × 317 mm ($14\frac{9}{16}$ × $12\frac{1}{2}$ ins.)

PROVENANCE: L.D. 125

Two sketches for the Ghost in *The Banquet Scene, Macbeth* (see cat. no. 84).

86 A Foregathering of Witches (1)

Grey watercolour wash and black ink wash-over pencil
394 × 521 mm ($15\frac{1}{2}$ × $21\frac{1}{2}$ ins.)

PROVENANCE: L.D. 47

The cavernous impression created in this rather theatrical setting does not really suggest the *Cavern Scene, Macbeth*. This composition has nothing to do with the incidents from the same scene which John Romney included in his gift to the Fitzwilliam. Later developments of the same composition show that witches dancing about a fire or cauldron are the main theme (see cat. nos. 87–9). Romney's general interest in witchcraft from 1789 onwards, and his particular interest in *Macbeth*, which seems to have intensified after the death of Reynolds in 1792, suggest a date in the early 1790s for these sheets.

87 A Foregathering of Witches (2)

Grey and black watercolour wash over pencil
381 × 572 mm (15 × $22\frac{1}{2}$ ins.)

PROVENANCE: L.D. 45

See cat. no. 86. The witches about the cauldron, massed as monumental shapes which become even more abstract as the composition progresses (see cat. nos. 88 and 89), may be contrasted with pen drawings of hags about a cauldron in the Folger sketch-book 'Macbeth / Midsummernight dream / McBeth' (fols. 37, 38, 44, 45).

88 A Foregathering of Witches (3)

Grey watercolour wash and black ink wash over pencil
397 × 546 mm (15$\frac{5}{8}$ × 21$\frac{1}{2}$ ins.)

PROVENANCE: L.D. 49

See notes on cat. no. 86. The dancing hags are now even more abstract than
they were in cat. no. 87.

89 A Foregathering of Witches (4)

Grey watercolour wash and black ink wash over pencil
397–394 × 518 mm (15$\frac{5}{8}$–15$\frac{1}{2}$ × 21$\frac{3}{8}$ ins.)

PROVENANCE: L.D. 48

See cat. no. 86. The tree at the left has disappeared, but this is sufficiently like
the other sketches for the subject to be associated with them without reserve.
The elements of the composition have now been reduced to an almost complete abstraction. The almost frenzied speed of working is typical of Romney
in the mid to late 1790s.

90 Landscape

Grey watercolour wash and grey ink wash over pencil
397 × 546 mm (15$\frac{5}{8}$ × 21$\frac{1}{2}$ ins.)

PROVENANCE: L.D. 51

This has the air of being a real landscape sketch. At the same time, with its
theatrically leaning tree at the right it reverses the general landscape composition for *A Foregathering of witches*, cat. nos. 86–9.

91 Meeting of the three witches and Hecate

Pen with black ink and grey watercolour wash over pencil
392 × 516 mm (15$\frac{7}{16}$ × 20$\frac{5}{8}$ ins.)
Verso: inscribed in ink '141'

PROVENANCE: B.V. 141

Identified by John Romney as being from *Macbeth*, Act III, sc. v. Cat. nos.
86–9 could have been intended to illustrate a meeting of witches such as this.

92   Queen Mab

Pencil and grey watercolour wash over pencil
386 × 538 mm ($15\frac{3}{16}$ × $21\frac{3}{16}$ ins.)
Verso: pencil, two composition trials for the same subject. Inscribed in ink
'No. 49'

PROVENANCE: B.V. 149

John Romney identifies these compositions as 'slight sketches of Titania and
her Fairies' (J.R. 266) his presumption being that the subject comes from
A Midsummer-night's Dream. However, the 'Titania' compositions in the
Folger sketch-book inscribed by Romney 'Midsummernight dream' are all
for the painting in which Emma modelled as Titania, curled up beneath a
canopy of low hanging leaves, a small baby at her side. The present composition compares with ones in the Folger sketch-book inscribed 'Queen
Mab'. The ominous, rather sinister quality of these versions of the fairy
theme may have been influenced by Fuseli's work. Johnson had commissioned him to illustrate a collected works of Milton to be edited by
William Cowper. Romney was obviously aware of this, as he wrote about it
to Hayley (W.H. 166). By 1791 the 34-year-old William Blake was also
established in the same circles. That year Romney painted Blake's political
hero Tom Paine, by that time a firebrand. Thomas Clio Rickman lists the
few London friends whom Paine dared to visit: 'Lord Edward Fitzgerald;
the French and American Ambassadors, Mr Sharp the engraver, Romney the
painter, Mrs Wolstonecroft, . . .' (Thomas Clio Rockman: *The Life of Tom
Paine* (London 1819) pp. 100–1). Romney must have felt that he was, like
David whom he admired in France, getting close to the political centre of
things. Perhaps as a result Blake's work made a greater impression on him.

93   Fairies

Pencil
249 × 192 mm ($9\frac{13}{16}$ × $7\frac{9}{16}$ ins.)

PROVENANCE: M.D. 39

The quality of pencil and energy of drawing differ from those of cat. no. 92,
but the concept of slightly derisive figures standing from left to left centre is
much the same. Another possibility is that this is a sketch for Joan of Arc's
fiends – the energy and rapidity of drawing being similar (see B.V. 132);
however, all Joan's fiends lay their fingers to their lips as an injunction to
silence, while the gesture of the foremost of the present figures corresponds
more closely with that of a 'fairy' in cat. no. 92. John Romney's identification
of subjects in this area are rather uncertain.

94 Figures in a Lazaretto

Pen with brown ink and brown ink wash over pencil
349–352 × 298–295 mm (13$\frac{3}{4}$–13$\frac{7}{8}$ × 11$\frac{3}{4}$–11$\frac{5}{8}$ ins.)
Verso: pencil; sketch, trimmed at left for composition similar to B.V. 156
(*Howard visiting a Lazaretto*); inscribed in pencil '38' and 'a'

PROVENANCE: L.D. 90

While Romney worked on Shakespearean subjects and revived a whole
series of pictures featuring the returned Emma, he was also constantly
meditating on the 'scenes of human wretchedness' reported in Howard's
surveys of prisons and lazarettos. This is an early version on the theme: later
the idea of an architectural setting framed the groups in dungeon gloom. The
compositions probably do not illustrate particular incidents, but are general-
ized pictures of the miseries of pestilence ridden lazarettos.

95 Howard visiting a lazaretto

Pen with brown ink and brown ink wash over pencil
363–371 × 537–541 mm (14$\frac{5}{16}$–14$\frac{5}{8}$ × 21$\frac{1}{8}$–21$\frac{5}{16}$ ins.)
Verso: inscribed '35' and 'Howd'

PROVENANCE: L.D. 89

This seems to develop the idea started in cat. no. 94, Howard and the jailor
at the left are surrounded by suffering and pleading inmates of the lazaretto.
Elements of this composition, though none is identical, reappear in B.V. 152
(cat. no. 96), B.V. 155, B.V. 156 and B.V. 157. Compare also L.D. 88. A
sketch-book, broken up, probably in the 1920s, by F. R. Meatyeard, contained compositions very close to the present and also sketches for the
Banquet scene, Macbeth: their probable date is therefore 1791–2.

96 Howard visiting a lazaretto

Pen with brown ink and grey-brown wash over traces of pencil, strengthened with black chalk
375 × 556 mm (14$\frac{3}{4}$ × 21$\frac{7}{8}$ ins.)
Verso: inscribed in ink 'No. 121' (deleted)

PROVENANCE: B.V. 152

See cat. no. 95. John Romney was obviously unsure how many pictures his
father planned on this subject. In the MS list presented to the Fitzwilliam
with his gift he notes, 'These 9 sketches were studies for two or three large

pictures, wch. Mr R. intended to have painted. . . .' By 1830 when his *Memoir* of his father was printed, the statement had been modified – 'These nine sketches were studies for one or two large pictures which Mr Romney intended to have painted.'

97 Howard visiting a lazaretto

Pen with brown ink and grey ink wash over pencil
357×424 mm ($14\frac{1}{16} \times 18$ ins.), roughly torn at left
Verso: pencil, brief scribbles for a composition in which the group at the left is the same as cat. no. 94

PROVENANCE: B.V. 157

See notes on cat. no. 94–6. Elements which occur in the right half of this composition also occur in Fitzwilliam B.V. 156.

98 Howard visiting a lazaretto

Pen and grey ink, grey watercolour wash and ink wash over pencil, strengthened on top with pencil
359×495 mm ($14\frac{1}{8} \times 19\frac{1}{2}$ ins.)
Verso: pencil, sketch for same subject: with kneeling woman at centre and bending, lamenting figures at right; it relates to B.V. 157 (cat. no. 97) and B.V. 160. There was the same group with the kneeling woman in the ex-Kenneth Garlick sketch-book (see notes to cat. no. 99) fol. 17

PROVENANCE: B.V. 153

See notes on cat. no. 99. The style and medium of the drawings are those associated with preparation for print making.

99 Howard visiting a lazaretto

Pen with black ink and grey watercolour wash over traces of pencil; strengthened on top with pencil

PROVENANCE: B.V. 154

LITERATURE: Crookshank, repr. plate 17

The development of this particular composition could be traced in a sketchbook formerly in the collection of Kenneth Garlick (sold Sotheby's and subsequently broken up in the summer of 1963). It was dated on the front cover 'August 1792'. On fols 11 *recto*, 11 *verso*, 12, 13 and 14 were sketches for this composition, but in reverse. On fols. 14 *verso*, 15 and 16 there were sketches in the same sense as the present composition. In the Fitzwilliam Museum sketch-book inscribed 'August 92/Milton/ Flood' (No. 3688) there is one isolated drawing on a Howard subject and it is for the present composition, every figure element being present. It is as though the Fitzwilliam sketch-book had been used to reverse one of the drawings in the ex-Kenneth Garlick sketch-book before enlarging it to the scale of this wash drawing. The style and medium of this drawing are those associated with preparation for print making.

100a Howard visiting a lazaretto

Pencil
121 × 172 mm (4¾ × 6¾ ins.)

PROVENANCE: M.D. 32a

This is a trimmed fragment from a sketch-book and shows how Romney worked on the Howard subjects in the later years of his preoccupation with the theme. Here the architecture is described in heavy low arches which give the whole a claustrophobic horror. The composition is worked in an almost frenzied mass of heavy dark pencil shadings. Often Romney seems to have been unaware when the lead had worn down so much that the wood was scoring into the paper. His eyesight may have deteriorated significantly.

It would be a long job to list all comparable Howard drawings from sketch-books. There are so many trimmed fragments among the mounted drawings purchased for the Fitzwilliam in 1874, that we can assume a sketch-book to have been broken up. Two more pages, probably from the same sketch-book, were on the London art market in 1968 (sold Christie's 12 November 1968, lot 154): one was of exactly the same composition and in the same technique as the present leaf. On the basis of Truro No. 3 (inscribed within the front cover 'May 1794') this composition should be dated 1794. The same nude figure of a woman lying on her back in the foreground occurs in the Truro sketch-book (sold Christie's 22 February 1966, lot 22), fols. 5, 7, 9, 11.

100b Howard visiting a lazaretto

Pencil
109 × 175 mm (4⁵⁄₁₆ × 6⅞ ins.)

PROVENANCE: M.D. 32b

A trimmed page from a sketch-book. See notes on cat. no. 100a.

Immersed in subjects of enchantment, witchcraft and horror, working with passion and intensity, full of high hopes that democracy and freedom would be launched in France and spread throughout Europe, secretly delighted to have painted Tom Paine and to be close to the centre of new political ferment, the nervous, ailing and enthusiastic Romney might have collapsed far sooner under the pressure of events had it not been for his friends. There was always his constant friend from the Dendron school, Thomas Greene. There was the ever ingratiating Hayley. Then, in 1791 Madame de Genlis and Pamela arrived.

In Paris in 1790 Romney, Hayley and Carwardine had received very kindly and helpful attention from Madame de Genlis, Governess to the children of the Duc d'Orléans. She it was who had taken them to see the Orléans collection, and a fine and exclusive religious house (W.H. 146–7). By the autumn of 1791 the Revolution had taken such an ominous hold in France that the wise governess travelled to England. With her came Pamela, her adopted daughter, widely thought to be her own child by the Duc d'Orléans. Naturally Hayley and Romney both offered the ladies entertainment. In the early months of 1792 Romney saw much of them in London. They shared his passion for the theatre, and in January 1792 Romney frequently accompanied them to the playhouse (W.H. 169). In January he also painted Madame de Genlis's portrait, and began at least two portraits of Pamela (see letter to Hayley 28 January 1792, W.H. 169). About Pamela he wrote with an enthusiasm matched only by that he had had for Emma. Again he had as model a beautiful young girl of about sixteen. Brought up in France, she must have seemed fascinatingly different from the English ladies who generally sat to him. In the British Museum there is a manuscript list in Hayley's autograph of letters from Romney. In January and February 1792 the letters are all about Madame de Genlis (referred to under her maiden name as 'M. Sillery') and Pamela: 'Jan 24: Account of M. Sillery & Pamela – Romney attends them three times to the play – Jan.: account of the pictures he is painting of Pamela. Fev. 27: excuses for not writing – his F. visiters (sic). *Winter:* His going to a new tragedy with M. Sillery &c. – Pamela's sitting— a kind letter and invitation to Naples from Lady Hamilton.' (British Museum Add. MS 30805.) It seems likely that he painted and drew Pamela more than he normally would a portrait sitter (see cat. nos. 101–3).

Their visits certainly cheered him. They too had moved in the same circles as Romney and Tom Paine. Indeed in December that year Pamela was to marry Lord Edward Fitzgerald, one of the few people Paine could visit during his last stay in London (see cat. no. 92 above). So far Democrats had not been disillusioned.

But Romney needed more than the support from friends, however cheering. He often felt depressed, and suffered from bilious and nervous disorders. As long ago as 1788 he had tried leaving the smoke of central London for the fresher air of Hampstead. On 21 April 1788 Hayley wrote to his wife 'Romney found himself so much oppressed by the London air that we have been with him to hunt for a lodging at Hampstead & have at last fixed him in a very quiet & snug little house with a good elderly woman alone in it – He means to sleep there & return to business early every morning.' (Fitzwilliam Museum Hayley papers XIX.) However, before the week was up the weather turned cold and wet, forcing Romney to give up the experiment and return shivering home (Fitzwilliam Museum Hayley papers XIX, William Hayley to Eliza Saturday 26 April 1788).

We do not know if the experiment of sleeping regularly above the London smog was tried again before 1793. The Rev. James Stainer Clarke wrote to Hayley on 28 June 1793, 'Our dear Friend Romney has taken a seven and sixpenny Lodging near Kilburn Wells – where he breakfasts and designs every Morning – he is waited upon by some beautiful little Children – and as his Landlord is a Nursery Man – he sees all kind of flowers in Perfection: but you will be more delighted when you know the Name of the House. It is very newly built, and the Proprietor being a Gardener, thought it characteristic to place in large letters near the top of his House

PINE Apple Place.'

(Fitzwilliam Museum, Hayley papers VI)

This time, thanks to the charms of the family, the experiment worked. On 18 July 1793 Romney himself wrote to Hayley 'I continue to go to my little villa to breakfast, and make designs every morning, which has been a delightful relief this hot weather. I have eight children to wait on me, and fine ones. I begin to feel the necessity of having these innocent little spirits about one, they give more soft delight to the mind than I can describe to soften the steps down declining life.' (Chamberlain 187) In the Fitzwilliam there are many sheets of puzzling drawings showing women and children, children at play and even obvious working class kitchen scenes. A selection of them are given here (cat. nos. 104–12). Some are inscribed on the back 'P'. At one time I thought this might mean they were the work of Romney's last pupil, Isaac Pocock. However, I now accept them all as the work of Romney and suppose that the 'P' may stand for 'Pine Apple Place'. This would also account for a group of late drawings being so uncharacteristic of Romney's other work.

101   Head of Pamela

Pencil

511 × 311 mm (20$\frac{1}{8}$ × 12$\frac{1}{4}$ ins.)

Verso: charcoal, childish scribbles – faces, flowers, diamond patterns and notes of music

PROVENANCE: L.D. 57

EXHIBITED: Kenwood, 1961, no. 45

Pamela, as one can see from the portrait of her reproduced by Gamlin (Hilda Gamlin, *George Romney and his art*, London 1894 facing p. 236), wore her hair in the fashionable French manner, cut short and sometimes bunched with a scarf about her head; her nose was straight and her mouth small with full lips. She was small built. Whereas Elizabeth Warren (cat. nos. 11–14) had been a very mature seventeen year old, Pamela looked too young for a girl of almost sixteen. In age and hair style the portraits of Pamela are comparable to the so-called *Parson's Daughter* (Tate Gallery), an unidentified portrait given this fanciful title when in the Anderdon collection (W. & R. II, 189).

102 Seated girl: possibly Pamela

Pencil
$367 \times 328 - 333$ mm ($14\frac{7}{16} \times 12\frac{15}{16} - 13\frac{1}{8}$ ins.)
Verso: pencil; scribbled crowd in mid-distance at right watching foreground standing figure at left (trimmed away at left). Possibly for *The Banquet Scene, Macbeth*; inscribed in pencil '65' and 'JP' lower right

PROVENANCE: L.D. 66

See general notes above and cat. no. 101. Alternatively this could, in view of the inscription on the back, be a drawing of one of the inhabitants of Pine Apple Place.

103 Portrait sketch of a girl

Pencil
$448 - 451 \times 256$ mm ($17\frac{5}{8} - 17\frac{3}{4} \times 10\frac{1}{16}$ ins.)
Verso: inscribed in pencil '56' and 'P'

PROVENANCE: L.D. 67

See general notes above and cat. no. 101. From the style and the age of the sitter this could be a sketch of Pamela with her hair bound up in a scarf. Alternatively it could be a young girl drawn at Pine Apple Place.

104 Seated woman

Pen with brown ink and brown wash over traces of pencil
$333 - 335 \times 257$ mm ($13\frac{1}{8} - 13\frac{1}{4} \times 10\frac{1}{8}$ ins.)
Verso: inscribed in pencil 'P'

PROVENANCE: L.D. 36

In view of the inscription and the style of drawing this could be a sketch made at Pine Apple Place. The very neo-classical element could be a direct result of Flaxman's return to England: in August 1794 Romney wrote to Hayley 'Though he is not here in person, I have caught a portion of his soul from the beautiful images of his Homer and Dante. I am charmed with them, they have thrown a light upon my mind, that has dissipated some of its thick gloom' (Chamberlain 194).

105   Mother and child playing with a doll

Brush with brown ink
303–301 × 244 mm ($11\frac{15}{16}$–$11\frac{7}{8}$ × $9\frac{5}{8}$ ins.)
Verso: brown ink; two sketches for standing figures; inscribed in pencil 'FP'

PROVENANCE: L.D. 28

See general notes above.

106   Three sketches of children

Brush with brown watercolour wash over pencil
384 × 451–445 mm ($15\frac{1}{8}$ × $17\frac{3}{4}$–$17\frac{1}{2}$ ins.)

PROVENANCE: L.D. 20

See general notes above.

107   Two women with two children

Brush with brown watercolour wash over pencil
373–381 × 381–384 mm ($14\frac{11}{16}$–15 × 15–$15\frac{1}{8}$ ins.)
Verso: pencil, slight sketches of three women

PROVENANCE: L.D. 21

See general notes above.

108   Woman and child in a kitchen

Pencil
392–387 × 436–445 mm ($15\frac{7}{16}$–$15\frac{1}{4}$ × $17\frac{3}{16}$–$17\frac{1}{2}$ ins.)

PROVENANCE: L.D. 31

See general notes above.

109   Woman, child and monkey

Brush with dark brown watercolour wash over pencil
336 × 229 mm ($13\frac{1}{4}$ × 9 ins.)

PROVENANCE: L.D. 30

See general notes above.

110 Two young girls talking

Brush with dark brown watercolour wash over pencil
346×213 mm (13⅝×8⅜ ins.)
Verso: inscribed in pencil 'P'

PROVENANCE: L.D. 25

'P' on the *verso* may refer to Pine Apple Place: see general notes.

111 Woman with large pan or basket

Brush with dark brown watercolour wash over pencil
345–343×259–265 mm (13$\frac{9}{16}$–13½×10$\frac{3}{16}$–10$\frac{7}{16}$ ins.)

PROVENANCE: L.D. 37

See general notes above.

112 Woman with toddling child

Brush with dark brown watercolour wash over pencil
281×264–267 mm (11$\frac{1}{16}$×10⅜–10½ ins.)

PROVENANCE: L.D. 27

See general notes above.

Despite the refreshing air and company which he enjoyed at Pine Apple Place, Romney's general health and spirits continued to worsen. External factors did not improve matters. His *Tempest* picture hung in the Boydell Gallery, but was not a popular success. Reynolds's *Macbeth and the Witches* hung there too, but with such lack of brilliance that the devoted Northcote, Reynolds's pupil and biographer hurried over it in three lines (James Northcote: *Memoirs of Sir Joshua Reynolds* (London 1813) p. 338). Romney, who had made splendid compositions on the theme of the witches, and Macbeth's meeting with them, must have felt doubly frustrated. Yet new plans were formed close on the heels of old endeavours. The Boydell Shakespeare Gallery only served to stimulate English publishers to promote other huge ventures. We have already seen how Henry Fuseli and William Cowper were involved in a projected edition of Milton (cat. no. 92). William Hayley, as ever chameleon-like, began to write a *Life of Milton*, and contacted Cowper on the pretext that their interests were mutual. True to form, Hayley lost no time in yoking Romney to the Milton scheme; true to form, Romney chose to work in a private frenzy. In a letter to John dated 4 February 1792 Romney had written, 'I have made, and am making designs from Milton; and mean to make several before I begin to paint them, but it is quite *a secret*' (J.R. 223). Then in the late summer he met at Eartham, as fellow guest, the sensitive, sympathetic William Cowper. Their conversation was chiefly of Milton, and in the evenings Cowper and Hayley worked on a joint translation of Andreini's *Adamo* – described by Romney as 'an Italian play on the subject of Satan' (J.R. 226). When he returned to London Romney's head must have been full of scenes from *Paradise Lost, Paradise Regained* and satanism. Earlier in the year he had painted Tom Paine, whom some saw as the devil incarnate: a contemporary newspaper reported 'Romney is said to be painting *Tom Paine*; but whether for an individual likeness or the hero of *Paradise Lost*, is not yet known. Those, however, who have seen the sketch of it, say it is *devilish* like' (W. & R. II, 115). The Radicals' hopes for the situation in France were still at that time high. But over the summer the situation deteriorated rapidly. On 8 September Romney wrote to Hayley from London 'I arrived here safe, but cannot say much for my health. Many unpleasant professional circumstances rushing upon my mind, may perhaps have operated too strongly on my frame. In a little time when more familiarized with the drudgery of my profession, my health may be better.

The accounts today from France are dreadful: all the priests that were confined are murdered, perhaps the city of Paris is at this time in flames. I am so agitated with the tremendous situation of that poor Country, I am not able to do anything' (W.H. 184).

The news from France was filled with massacre and brutality and Romney seems to have been in possession of detailed accounts quite rapidly. The sketchbook formerly in the collection of Kenneth Garlick (dated on the cover 'August 1792'), has an account in Romney's hand of the massacre of the Swiss guard at the Tuileries on 10 August 1792. It is evident from his account that at that stage his sympathies were still with the Revolution. The report came from an aristocrat who had declared that 'it is a Government of Blackguards – and I find from his account', wrote Romney, 'that all are Blackguards except them that are *born gentlemen* – so you see I am amongst the Blackguards – and I hope to God that they will prevail—' (formerly fols. 23 *verso* and 23). Even on 10 October 1792 he could still write to his son 'The extraordinary events that here succeeded each other for the last three months past has (*sic*) interested and astonished the world in a very high degree: the present moment is an epock (*sic*) in Liberty that has never happened before since the Creation – I confess the Sublimity of it taking it together has interested and agitated me much.' (ALS George Romney to his son 10 October 1792, Fitzwilliam Museum Cambridge. The letter was purchased in 1941 with a fine uncut copy in printer's boards of Hayley's *Life and Posthumous Writings of William Cowper*. An abridged and otherwise slightly doctored version of this letter is printed by John Romney: *Memoirs of George Romney* pp. 225–6. The above passage is one of those omitted.) By this time, perhaps, his system of news bulletins was moving more slowly. With the September Massacres had begun the first pathetic processions to the guillotine. Monarchy was abolished and on 21 January 1793 Louis XVI was executed: the Reign of Terror had begun. Romney's faith in the liberalising effect of the Revolution was shaken. Always a nervous man, he appears to have felt the events in France so deeply that the very atmosphere of mob violence seemed to close in about him. The London crowd seemed menacing. In September 1793 he confided in Hayley that returning from Eartham, 'the approach to London affected me in various ways. I

66

observed a sharpness of countenance in the people I met: with passions so strongly marked, I suppose none could mistake. Deep design, disappointed ambition, envy, hatred, melancholy, disease and poverty. These appearances one is forever meeting on the skirts of London' (W.H. 204).

In his drawings from 1792 onwards we can trace the growing intensity of his hopes and fears. After 1793 the disappointment and disillusionment of his political hopes and artistic ambitions plunged him into deeper and deeper depression. Hayley was still urging the Howard subjects upon him: on 5 January 1793 Romney wrote thanking him for 'kindness in sending me descriptions of the picturesque prison scenes which will produce new ideas in my mind' (W.H. 196). The following year he was still working on Howard subjects and on several from Milton 'three where Satan is the hero, and three of Adam and Eve'. Moreover he had 'formed a plan of painting the Seven Ages, and also the Vision of Adam with the Angel, to bring in the flood, and the opening of the ark . . . (but this is a profound secret)' (George Romney to William Hayley from Pine Apple Place 15 February 1794, W.H. 212).

Not only were affairs in France tragic, but these years held personal griefs for Romney. The death of Reynolds marked the passing of an epoch. Any fantasies that Romney may have had of taking his place as the leader of English art when his greatest rival had gone, were naturally dashed. He was at the melancholy age when a man watches his own generation, with aspirations unfulfilled, fading away. His physician friend, Dr Austen, died (Bishop 171). William Cowper was relapsing into insanity. Romney was deeply shocked by the news and was eager for any ray of hope that sanity would return: 'if there is a situation more deplorable than any other in nature, it is the horrible decline of reason, and the derangement of that power we have been blessed with. How hard it is for a man with a feeling mind to preserve that balance in his understanding, that carries him well through life.' (George Romney to William Hayley from Pine Apple Place, 18 October 1794, W.H. 223–4.) Romney, always on the brink of nervous disorders himself, spoke from the heart. He was now in a depression so profound that he hardly recognised it: on 13 September that year he had written to Hayley, 'To divert my mind a little I have begun the first stage of man, and the prison scene.' (W.H. 220) The drawings he made of the subjects were desperately dark visions of pain and suffering (cat. nos. 100 and 101). The *Birth of Man* itself seems to take place in a prison (cat. no. 123).

Visits to Eartham in the summer, and breakfast at Pine Apple Place during his working months in London, were the only things which now could relieve his spirits. Expert analysis by an historically sensitive psychologist is needed to unravel the intricate convolutions of Romney's life and work in these last years of his career. Probably Eartham and Pine Apple Place offered some relief from his worries, because going there he had a sense of escape. If so, he did not realise the significance. He himself took the step which robbed him of the recreation of escape. He decided to build a place for himself in Hampstead. In this studio he planned to arrange all the casts of the antique which Flaxman had been commissioned to acquire for him in Rome. In January 1793 Romney was able to report to Hayley 'My plaster figures are unpacked, and I am charmed with them, both for the choice, and the perfection of the casts. I shall have one of the finest Museums in London for antique sculpture' (W.H. 197). He began to study the casts intensively, planning how they should populate his projected studio, and how best he should animate them. The effects must have been weird. John Romney reports: 'Mr Romney had great pleasure in studying and contemplating these casts; and I have known him sometimes have evening parties in his private painting-room, when he suspended a powerful lamp over the Laocoon, which, by its descending rays, gave a bold relief to the muscles and prominences of the figures, and a terrific grandeur to the group altogether, approaching to something like reality' (J.R. 233). We glimpse the bizarre: Romney nervous and depressed, filling his lonely house with the gigantic contorted shadows of life-sized plaster casts, lit unsteadily by lamps. By 1796 his whole attention seems to have become fixed on the plans for his new house. John Romney, viewing it all as a waste of money, was not pleased: 'When I visited Mr Romney in 1796 I found him occupied in making plans of fantastic buildings, instead of studies for pictures as heretofore. It was evident that his mind was thrown off its pivot, and that painting had lost its influence.' (J.R. 250.) He was, though he did not realise it, planning his own prison. 'In 1797 and 1798 . . . he raised a whimsical structure, consisting chiefly of a picture and statue gallery; but with few domestic accommodations. . . . Hither he removed at Christmas, 1798, before the walls were dry.' (J.R. 251) Naturally it was all too much for him. John Romney suspected he had already suffered from a slight stroke before the move. The new studio did not prove an escape, but rather a trap: his depression intensified. Hayley 'found Romney much dejected in his new mansion on the hill of Hampstead, for want of occupation and society' (W.H. 284).

Romney had to escape. In 1799 he took the unusual step of making a winter visit to Hayley at Eartham (W.H. 291). He stayed from 7 February to 6 March, and seemed to benefit from the change. He returned to Hampstead. But before the summer was out he had again to escape: this time he went north, returning at last to be nursed by his long neglected wife. His working life was over. He died on 15 November 1802, a month before his sixty-eighth birthday. The chaos of drawings and unfinished paintings which he left in London still presents a welter of enigmas.

113   Coven of witches

Pencil
136×213 mm (5⅜×8⅜ ins.)
Verso: Inscribed in pencil '45' and 'Lapland' (not Romney's autograph)

PROVENANCE: M.D. 2

A leaf from a sketch-book. Compare M.D. 1a, M.D. 1b and M.D. 11a. Fundamentally the same composition as L.D. 154, M.D. 1b shows a hag at the left, brandishing a flaming torch above her head. It may be a later interpretation of the subject *Joan of Arc upon the walls of Rouen* (cat. no. 83). These drawings, if they are to be associated with Joan of Arc, may be expressive of Romney's sense of the worsening situation in France as the Revolution progressed.

114 Fall of the Rebel Angels

Pen with black ink and grey watercolour wash over pencil
540 × 391–386 mm (21¼ × 15⅜–15 3/16 ins.)
Verso: inscribed in brown ink 'No. 143'

PROVENANCE: B.V. 161

The *Fall of the Rebel Angels* is an incident in Milton's *Paradise Lost*, Book I,
Satan . . .

> 'Against the throne and monarchy of God
> Raised impious war in Heaven, and battle proud,
> With vain attempt Him the Almighty Power
> Hurl'd headlong, flaming from the ethereal sky,
> With hideous ruin and combusion, down
> To bottomless perdition, there to dwell
> In adamantine chains and penal fire,
> Who durst defy the Omnipotent to arms.'

This drawing is carefully worked up in parts. The left arm of 'the Almighty Power' has been sketched in in ink as raised to balance with the right arm, then deleted with dark grey watercolour wash and finally drawn over the watercolour in gouache, showing it down at his side.

The sketches for this subject are very numerous. Those in the Fitzwilliam include B.V. 162–4, and M.D.s 18, 58a, 58b, 59, 61a, 63c, 64b and 69.

John Romney identifies the composition as 'the last Mr Romney ever made'. Stylistically this is doubtful, although they do belong to his last years.

115 Satan *for* The Fall of the Rebel Angels

Pen with dark grey ink and grey wash over pencil, plus two sketches in pencil alone
537 × 384 mm (21⅛ × 15⅛ ins.)
Verso: inscribed in ink 'No. 140' (cancelled)

PROVENANCE: B.V. 163

See notes on cat. no. 115. The figure of Satan should be compared with Richard Westall's illustrations for *Paradise Lost*, Book IV. The separate pencil sketches at the upper right are for 'the Almighty Power' and should be compared with Westall's depiction of God in *Paradise Lost*, Book VI. Both plates after Westall were published on 4 June 1794 as illustrations to Boydell and Nicol's *Poetical Works of John Milton* (London 1794). This particular watercolour drawing should be compared particularly with the pencil sketch M.D. 59.

116   Head of Satan *for* The Fall of the Rebel Angels

Pencil

187×159 mm (7$\frac{3}{8}$×6$\frac{1}{4}$ ins.)

PROVENANCE: M.D. 69

See cat. no. 114. This appears to be another head study made with Hayley as the basic model.

117a   The Temptation of Christ

Pencil

120×119 mm (4$\frac{3}{4}$×4$\frac{11}{16}$ ins.)

PROVENANCE: M.D. 51a

A trimmed fragment from a sketch-book. The large painting was never finished because Romney 'experienced some slight paralytic affection, which, I have no doubt, took place while he was engaged with the picture of *The Temptation of Christ*, and which consequently put a stop to that grand design' (J.R. 253). However, John Romney outlines his father's intention in the composition. 'Another great work, which he commenced about 1796, was *The Temptation of Christ*. Had he finished this picture, it would have ranked him with Michael Angelo. It was equal in original conception and wild fancy to anything ever produced by any artist. When one looked at Christ, silent passiveness was the idea which presented itself to the Spectator; when at the fiends that assailed him, vociferating noise and boisterous insult. These visionary beings were the human passions and appetites personified. To aid the malevolent purpose, the illusive representations, or ghosts of Eve and Noah, were called forth. And the arch-fiend, the Miltonic satan, grand as the human mind can conceive him, viewed from the upper corner of the picture, with malignant satisfaction, the ready obedience of his imps.' (J.R. 244–5.) There are many drawings for this subject in the Fitzwilliam collection. They are all in the category M.D., and are trimmed sketch-book fragments, possibly all from the same book as the present one. See also cat. nos. 117b, 118a, 118b and 119a.

117b   The Temptation of Christ

Pencil

132×165 mm (5$\frac{3}{16}$×6$\frac{1}{2}$ ins.)

PROVENANCE: M.D. 51b

A trimmed fragment from a sketch-book. See notes on cat. no. 117a. In this particular sketch there is a slight indication in the upper left corner of what

John Romney describes as 'the arch-fiend' who is viewing 'from the upper corner of the picture, with malignant satisfaction, the ready obedience of his imps' (J.R. 245). See cat. no. 119a.

118a   The Temptation of Christ

Pencil
128 × 160 mm (5$\frac{1}{16}$ × 6$\frac{1}{4}$ ins.)

PROVENANCE: M.D. 54a

A trimmed fragment from a sketch-book. See notes on cat. no. 117a.

118b   The Temptation of Christ

Pencil
131 × 184 mm (5$\frac{3}{16}$ × 7$\frac{1}{4}$ ins.)

PROVENANCE: M.D. 54b

A trimmed fragment from a sketch-book. See notes on cat. no. 117a.

119a   Head of Satan *for* The Temptation of Christ

Pencil
115 × 101 mm (4$\frac{1}{2}$ × 4 ins.)

PROVENANCE: M.D. 25a

A trimmed fragment from a sketch-book. See cat. no. 117b, where Satan is roughly indicated in the top left corner.

119b   Head of a man

Pencil
151 × 111 mm (5$\frac{15}{16}$ × 4$\frac{1}{2}$ ins.)

PROVENANCE: M.D. 25b

A character study for which William Hayley may have sat.

120   Head of a hag

Pencil
206×237 mm (8⅛×9⁵⁄₁₆ ins.)

PROVENANCE: M.D. 13

Probably an apparation for *The Temptation of Christ*. Compare M.D. 14.

121a   Satanic figure inflicting punishment

Pencil
114×116 mm (4½×4⁹⁄₁₆ ins.)

PROVENANCE: M.D. 41a

A trimmed fragment from a sketch-book. This powerful drawing is comparable to those in a sketch-book belonging to the Art Institute of Chicago. That now contains only sixteen leaves. It is possible that this fragment once formed part of the sketch-book, which contains a draft of the letter mentioned by Hayley as having been received 'in the summer of 1794' (W.H. 216). Comparable sketches are also to be found in a sketch-book formerly belonging to the De Pass collection, Royal Institute of Cornwall, Truro, and actually dated on the cover 'May 94'. (Sold Christie's 22 February 1966, lot 22.) A spread from this sketch-book was reproduced as end papers in the Smith catalogue – mistakenly identified as coming from a sketch-book in the Fitzwilliam Museum.

121b   The Ghost of Noah *for* the Temptation of Christ

Pencil
108×131 mm (4¼×5⅛ ins.)
Verso: pencil; another sketch for the same

PROVENANCE: M.D. 41b

A trimmed fragment from a sketch-book. See notes on cat. no. 117a.

122a   The Ghost of Noah *for* The Temptation of Christ

Pencil
94×100 mm (3¹¹⁄₁₆×3¹⁵⁄₁₆ ins.)

PROVENANCE: M.D. 44a

A trimmed fragment from a sketch-book. See notes on cat. no. 117a. Compare also M.D. 53a and M.D. 54b.

122b The Ghost of Noah *for* the Temptation of Christ

Pencil
109 × 130 mm ($4\frac{5}{16}$ × $5\frac{1}{8}$ ins.)

PROVENANCE: M.D. 44b

A trimmed fragment from a sketch-book. See notes on cat. no. 117a.

122c The Ghost of Noah *for* The Temptation of Christ

Pencil
109 × 130 mm ($4\frac{5}{16}$ × $5\frac{1}{8}$ ins.)

PROVENANCE: M.D. 44c

A trimmed fragment from a sketch-book. See notes on cat. no. 117a. The figure at the lower right might possibly represent Eve.

122d The Ghost of Noah *for* The Temptation of Christ

Pencil
107 × 126 mm ($4\frac{3}{16}$ × $4\frac{15}{16}$ ins.) lower corner trimmed diagonally

PROVENANCE: M.D. 44d

A trimmed fragment from a sketch-book. See notes on cat. no. 117a.

123 The Birth of Man

Pencil
114 × 156 mm ($4\frac{1}{2}$ × $6\frac{1}{8}$ ins.)

PROVENANCE: M.D. 71

A trimmed page from a sketch-book.

It was in 1793 that Romney wrote to Hayley, 'I have been arranging some of the subjects in the Seven Ages, and I think I shall be able to make some of them out soon' (Romney to Hayley from Pine Apple Place, 12 December 1793, quoted W.H. 208). Hayley admits that 'The favourite project of my friend, at this period, was to delineate, in a series of pictures, the whole life of man, and not to confine himself to Shakespeare's celebrated description of the different ages.' However, although this composition has little of Shake-'speare about it, it does not bear much resemblance to Hayley's description of the projected picture, the baby 'on the bosom of its reclining mother, whose couch is surrounded by several attendants, and among them her husband, a young man of florid health in the habiliments of a hunter, who seems eager to give a kiss of benediction to his wife and child before he sets forth for the chace. This picture like all its intended companions was never completed, though several parts of it, had exquisite expression, and beauty.' (W.H. 209.) There was in the Haas collection, Paris, an undated sketch-book cover inscribed on the marbled boards 'Birth of Man'. In 1927 and 1928 the Haas family sold a large selection of so-called 'Shakesperean drawings' to the Folgers through the New York dealer, Gabriel Wells. Among them, mounted in a large bound volume (1927 purchase) and in a smaller bound volume (1928 purchase) are about 69 trimmed sketch-book pages with versions of this *Birth of Man* composition – more than enough to have filled an empty sketch-book cover. All set the scene in a gloomy confined atmosphere, more like the Howard scenes than Hayley's happy description. The new-born infant sprawls across the knees of a crouching midwife figure while the pale mother reclines on a bed behind. It is a scene of agony. Nothing could speak more clearly of the pessimism of Romney's view of life in the 1790s.

REFERENCES

Bishop: Morchard Bishop, *Blake's Hayley, The Life, Works, and Friendships of William Hayley* [London, Gollancz, 1951]

Blake . . . Nonesuch: *The Complete Writings of William Blake with all the variant readings*, edited by Geoffrey Keynes [London, The Nonesuch Press, 1957]

B.V.:   Bound Volume which originally contained the 164 drawings given to the University in September 1818 by the painter's son, the Rev. John Romney of St John's College, Cambridge.

Chamberlain: Arthur B. Chamberlain, *George Romney* [London, Methuen & Co., 1910]

Christie's 1807:   *Catalogue of the Select and Reserved Collection of Paintings, of that eminent and very celebrated Artist, George Romney, Esq., R.A.* (sic) *deceased – consisting of the most admired Productions of his Pencil*, . . . Monday 27 April 1807.

Crookshank: Anne Olivia Crookshank, 'The Drawings of George Romney', *Burlington Magazine*, vol. XCIX, No. 647, February 1957, pp. 43–8.

J.R.:   John Romney, *Memoirs of the Life and Works of George Romney, including various letters, and testimonials to his genius, &c. also, some particulars of the life of Peter Romney, his brother*, . . . [London, Baldwin and Cradock, 1830]

Kenwood, 1961:   *George Romney, Paintings and Drawings*, the Iveagh Bequest, Kenwood (London County Council), 1961

Lady Hamilton 1972:   *Lady Hamilton in relation to the art of her time*, the Iveagh Bequest, Kenwood (Arts Council of Great Britain) 18 July–16 October 1972 – exhibition selected and catalogued by Patricia Jaffé.

L.D.:   Loose Drawings, purchased in the large acquisition, 2 May 1874 by the Fitzwilliam Museum.

M.D.:   Mounted drawings, purchased in the large acquisition, of 2 May 1874 by the Fitzwilliam Museum.

Portfolio: Portfolio of twelve drawings of the female nude, part of the block purchase 2 May 1874.

Smith College 1962:   *The Drawings of George Romney*, Smith College Museum of Art, Northampton, Mass. May–September

	1962 – exhibition selected and catalogued by Patricia Milne Henderson (Patricia Jaffé).
Sutherland Gower:	Lord Ronald Sutherland Gower, *George Romney* [London, Duckworth and Co., 1904]
Truro:	Sketch-book formerly in the De Pass Collection, Royal Institute of Cornwall, Truro.
W.H.:	William Hayley, *The Life of George Romney, Esq.* [Chichester; printed by W. Mason for T. Payne, Pall-Mall, London, 1809]
W. & R. I:	Humphrey Ward and W. Roberts, *Romney, a bio-*
W. & R. II:	*graphical and critical essay with a catalogue raisonné of his works*, 2 vols [London, Thomas Agnew and Sons, 1904]

Cat. No. 1a

Cat. No. 1b

Cat. No. 2

Cat. No. 2 verso

Cat. No. 4

Cat. No. 5

Cat. No. 6

Cat. No. 6 verso

Cat. No. 7

Cat. No. 7 verso

Cat. No. 10

Cat. No. 10 verso

Cat. No. 15

Cat. No. 15 verso

Cat. No. 19

Cat. No. 20

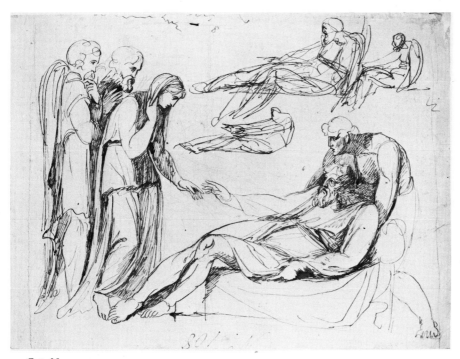

Cat. No. 20 verso

Cat. No. 22

Cat. No. 30

Cat. No. 31

Cat. No. 32

Cat. No. 35

Cat. No. 37

Cat. No. 38

Cat. No. 39

Cat. No. 40

Cat. No. 40 verso

Cat. No. 41

Cat. No. 43

Cat. No. 45

Cat. No. 46

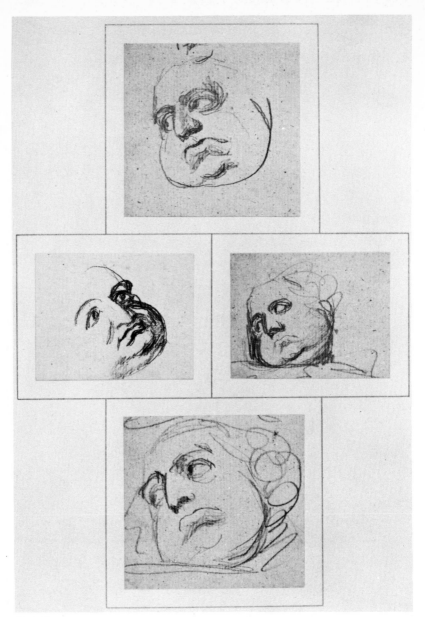

Cat. No. 47

Cat. No. 56

Cat. No. 57

Cat. No. 58

Cat. No. 59

Cat. No. 60

Cat. No. 61

Cat. No. 61 verso

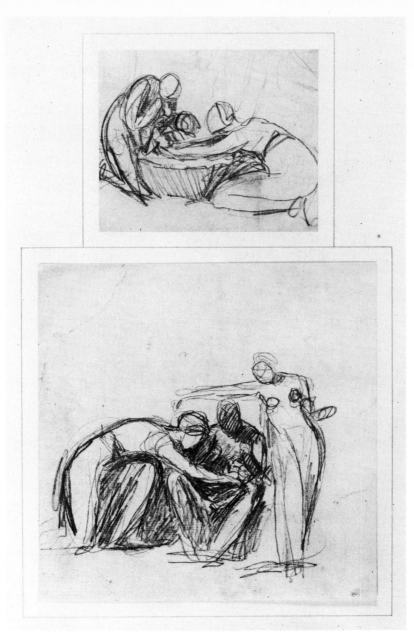

Cat. No. 62

Cat. No. 62 verso

Plate No. 29

Cat. No. 65 verso   Cat. No. 65

Cat. No. 66

Cat. No. 66 verso

Cat. No. 69

Cat. No. 70

Cat. No. 71

Cat. No. 78

Cat. No. 79

Cat. No. 79 verso

Plate No. 36

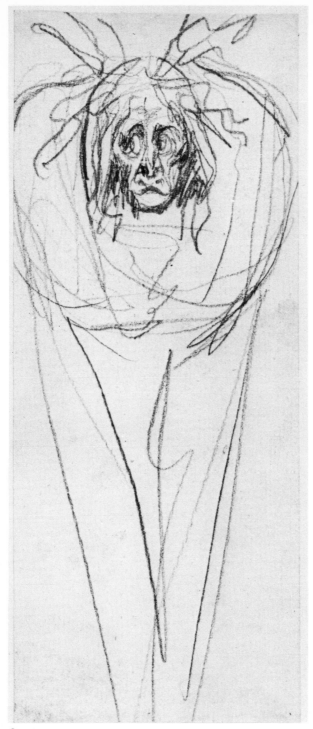

Cat. No. 80

Cat. No. 85

Cat. No. 87

Cat. No. 88

Cat. No. 89

Cat. No. 93

Cat. No. 97

Cat. No. 97 verso

Cat. No. 98

Cat. No. 98 verso

Cat. No. 99

Cat. No. 100(a)

Cat. No. 100(b)

Cat. No. 106

Cat. No. 107

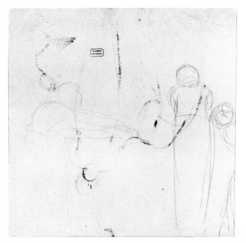

Cat. No. 107 verso

Plate No. 48

Cat. No. 108

Cat. No. 109

Cat. No. 110

Cat. No. 113

Cat. No. 114

Cat. No. 116

Cat. No. 117

Cat. No. 121

Cat. No. 121(b)

Cat. No. 123